The
Cupcake

The Cupcake

*Life's better with
a cupcake*

First published in 2011
LOVE FOOD is an imprint of Parragon Books Ltd

Parragon
Queen Street House
4 Queen Street
Bath BA1 1HE, UK

ISBN: 978-1-4454-3807-8

Printed in China

Introduction and new recipes by Angela Drake
Cover and internal photography by Clive Streeter
Home economy by Angela Drake and Teresa Goldfinch
Introduction design by Pink Creative

Notes for the Reader
This book uses both metric and imperial measurements. Follow the same units of
measurement throughout; do not mix metric and imperial. All spoon measurements are level:
teaspoons are assumed to be 5 ml, and tablespoons are assumed to be 15 ml. Unless otherwise
stated, milk is assumed to be whole, eggs are large, individual vegetables are medium, and
pepper is freshly ground black pepper.

The times given are an approximate guide only. Preparation times differ according to the
techniques used by different people and the cooking times may also vary from those given.
Optional ingredients, variations, or serving suggestions have not been included in the calculations.

Recipes using raw or very lightly cooked eggs should be avoided by infants, the elderly,
pregnant women, convalescents, and anyone with a chronic illness. Pregnant and breast-
feeding women are advised to avoid eating peanuts and peanut products. People with nut
allergies should be aware that some of the prepared ingredients used in the recipes in this
book may contain nuts. Always check the packaging before use.

Introduction

Who can resist the sweet and delicious charms of a cupcake? Easy to make, simple to decorate, and perfect for any occasion, the cupcake has become everyone's favorite cake!

From tiny bite-size miniature cupcakes or delicately decorated, dainty cupcakes to fabulously over-the-top frosted cakes or fun novelty cakes, cupcakes are incredibly versatile creations. Conveniently packaged in their own paper liners, they are certainly the simplest of all cakes to make, but, once decorated, they can become the star attraction for any celebration, from a children's birthday party to a wedding.

Making cupcakes is a joyful pastime for anyone, from the novice baker to the experienced cook, and for young children it's often their first experience of home baking—helping Mom to make a batch of cupcakes and then eagerly tasting the slightly awry results!

This book has absolutely everything you need to know about making and decorating cupcakes. It has a comprehensive introduction to cupcake making, including all the basic equipment and ingredients you will need, clear and descriptive steps for baking and frosting, as well as plenty of tips and ideas for fun and fancy decorations and perfect ways to display cupcakes or to give them as gifts.

Once you've mastered the basics, you can turn the pages and choose from any one of 80 divine cupcake recipes. From simple-to-make classic cupcakes to cute novelty designs, truly indulgent chocolate creations or elegantly decorated showstoppers, you really will be spoiled for choice. Welcome to the wonderful world of the cupcake!

Baking Equipment

The beauty of baking cupcakes is that you really don't need a lot of expensive or fancy equipment. Most of you will have the few necessary basics in your kitchen already. Here's a list of what you'll need to get started.

Measuring cups

Accurate measuring of ingredients is a major key to all successful baking. Transparent glass or plastic measuring pitchers are available for measuring liquids—choose ones wth clear markings and a pouring lip, and always check the measurements when at eye level. Dry measuring cups are available in nested sets and usually include 1-cup, ½-cup, ⅓-cup, and ¼-cup sizes. Ingredients should be placed in a measuring cup loosely, and, unless otherwise stated, the ingredients in the cups should be level—you can use the straight back of a knife to level them off.

Measuring spoons

Using a set of standard kitchen measuring spoons will ensure that small quantities of ingredients, such as baking powder, baking soda, and vanilla extract, are measured accurately. They are usually sold in sets of four, five, or six spoons and will measure out between ¼ teaspoon and 1 tablespoon. Always use a level spoonful, unless stated otherwise in the recipe.

Mixing bowls

Although you need only a large mixing bowl for making most cupcakes, it's useful to have a selection of two or three bowls in different sizes. Toughened and heatproof glass bowls are hard-wearing and practical. Ceramic bowls are available in a variety of colors and look attractive in the kitchen.

Sifters and strainers

To sift dry ingredients and remove any lumps, you will need a sifter, or you can use a large metal or plastic strainer with a medium to fine mesh. A sifter or a small fine-mesh strainer is also handy for decorating cupcakes with a dusting of unsweetened cocoa or confectioners' sugar. After washing metal equipment, make sure it is thoroughly dry before putting it away.

Baking Equipment

Spoons

You'll need wooden spoons for creaming and mixing, and a metal spoon for folding in ingredients. Wooden spoons are inexpensive to buy, so it's worth having a few in a range of sizes. Always make sure they are dried thoroughly after washing, and throw away any that are old or split. A good-size metal spoon is essential for the folding-in stage of cupcake making.

Electric mixer

Although not essential, an electric mixer makes light work of cupcake making, especially if you use the all-in-one method. Choose one with at least three variable-speed settings to avoid overbeating the batter.

Spatulas

A flexible rubber or silicone spatula is useful for light mixing of ingredients and for scraping down the batter from the sides of bowls. A spatula with a spoon-shaped tip is ideal for scooping up batter to fill pastry bags.

Muffin pans

To ensure even cooking and a good shape, cupcakes are best baked in metal or silicone muffin pans. They usually have 6 or 12 cups to sit paper liners in. Some metal pans have a nonstick coating, which is useful if you want to make cupcakes without paper liners. Flexible silicone liners come in a variety of bright colors and can also be used without paper liners.

The cup size in a standard muffin pan is 2½ inches/6 cm in diameter, but the cup sizes in muffin pans vary, from tiny ones ideal for miniature cupcakes to large, deep cups suitable for giant muffins. There are even a few muffin-top pans available, with 4-inch/10-cm-diameter cups that are only ½ inch/1 cm deep. The type of pan you use will affect the appearance of your cupcakes.

Wire cooling rack

Once baked, cupcakes need to be transferred to a wire rack to let them cool quickly and evenly. If you plan to make batches of cupcakes, it would be useful to invest in a tiered wire rack, which will save on taking up countertop space.

Decorating Equipment

Baking liners

You'll find a huge range of baking liners, also called baking cups, available in stores and online. As a general guide, here are the different sizes and styles of liners.

♡ **Jumbo baking liners**—these large, deep 3½-inch/9-cm-diameter liners are perfect for making giant cupcakes or for making muffins.

♡ **Standard baking liners**—these are smaller than the jumbo liners, with a diameter of about 2–2½ inches/5–6 cm, depending on the manufacturer, and they hold a little less batter.

♡ **Miniature baking liners**—the small cups are ideal for bite-size mini cupcakes.

♡ **The materials**—baking liners and cups are available in paper, foil, and silicone. Silicone cups are a fantastic modern invention and are available in a range of colors, sizes, and novelty designs. Most stand up by themselves so you won't need a muffin pan—just sit them on a baking sheet. The main advantage of using these is that they are reusable.

In every recipe in this book, you can use any size of liner but remember not to overfill them and adjust the cooking time accordingly.

Pastry bags and tips

For piping big swirls of cream or buttercream on top of cupcakes, choose either a large reusable plastic pastry bag or disposable plastic pastry bags. Both can be fitted with large star or plain tips.

For more intricate decorations, invest in a decorating kit that contains a small plastic-lined cloth pastry bag, a number of small metal decorating tips, and a coupler that lets you change tips without emptying the bag. Alternatively, buy a package of small silicone paper pastry bags or make your own from wax paper (see page 31).

Cutters

Round, plain or fluted cutters are ideal for stamping out rounds of fondant to top cupcakes. Small, shaped cutters (hearts, numbers, flowers, etc.) are great for simple but effective decorations.

Rolling pin

For rolling out small quantities of marzipan or fondant, it's worth buying a small nonstick rolling pin from a specialty cake decorating store.

Palette knives

To swirl frosting onto cupcakes, you'll need a medium-size palette knife. A small angled palette knife is also useful for lifting and placing fondant shapes or other decorations onto the top of cupcakes.

Food colorings

Food colorings are available in a variety of colors in either liquid or paste form. Pastes produce a good deep color and are best for coloring marzipan, fondant, and royal icing. Liquid colorings can be used for coloring glazes and buttercream. Look for pastes in a specialty cake decorating store.

Fun with shapes!

Ingredients

Butter or margarine

Lightly salted butter or soft margarine in a container can be used to make cupcakes, although butter will produce a richer and creamier flavor. Whichever you choose, remove it from the refrigerator at least 1 hour before starting to bake because it needs to be completely soft to be successfully creamed with the sugar. For the best flavor, use unsalted butter for buttercream.

Sugar

Superfine sugar has fine grains, making it ideal to cream smoothly with butter or margarine. If you can't find it in your local store, process granulated sugar in a food processor for about 1 minute. Brown sugar produces a darker cake with a richer caramel flavor. Confectioners' sugar, or powdered sugar, has a fine powdery texture and dissolves easily—perfect for frostings.

Flour

Most of the cupcake recipes in this book use self-rising flour. Always check that self-rising flour has not passed its expiration date, after which the leavening agent will be less effective. You can use all-purpose flour as a substitute if you add 1½ teaspoons of baking powder and ½ teaspoon of salt per 1 cup of flour. To incorporate as much air and lightness into the cupcake batter as possible, sift the flour before using. If using whole wheat flour, remember to tip any bran left in the sifter into the mixing bowl, because this is the most nutritious and flavorsome part.

Eggs

For the best baking results, always use fresh eggs at room temperature. If eggs are too cold, they will curdle the creamed butter-and-sugar batter. Be sure to use the correct egg size for the recipe—all the recipes in this book use large eggs, unless stated otherwise.

Leavening agents

Both baking powder and baking soda are used as leavening agents to produce light and airy cupcakes. Only buy in small quantities and check the expiration date before using.

Flavoring extracts

Vanilla and almond extracts—when used sparingly—can add a wealth of flavor to a simple cupcake batter, and other natural extracts, such as lemon, orange, and peppermint, are also available. For delicately scented cupcakes, invest in a small bottle of rose or orange flower water.

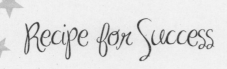

Recipe for Success

♡ Always preheat the oven for at least 15 minutes before you start baking. Because all ovens are different, use the temperature in the recipe as a guide. If your oven is a little hotter or colder, then adjust the temperature accordingly. An oven thermometer is useful, especially if you have an older oven that doesn't have a light indicating when the required temperature is reached. Convection ovens tend to be hotter than conventional ovens, so reduce the temperature by 25 degrees or follow the manufacturer's recommendations.

♡ Assemble all the ingredients and make sure that you have enough of each ingredient—you don't want to have to run out for another egg halfway through the recipe! Butter or margarine and eggs should be at room temperature. The butter should be of a soft, spreadable consistency.

♡ Make sure that all ingredients are carefully measured. Too much or too little of any one ingredient and you will have less than perfect results.

♡ Cream the butter and sugar thoroughly until the batter is very pale and fluffy. This will take at least 5 minutes by hand or 3–4 minutes with an electric mixer.

♡ Add the beaten eggs to the creamed batter about 1 tablespoonful at a time. Beat thoroughly after each addition to make sure all the egg has been incorporated before adding the next spoonful. If you add the egg too quickly, the batter will start to curdle. If the creamed batter does start to curdle, stir in a spoonful of the measured flour before adding more egg.

♡ Don't overmix when folding in the flour, otherwise you'll knock out all the air you've just beaten in! Use a light cutting-and-folding action and make sure to scoop up all the batter from the bottom of the bowl.

♡ If you follow the all-in-one method, the recipe will call for a little extra leavening agent to compensate for the air not being incorporated during the initial creaming stage. You'll need to use an electric mixer for this method and be careful to beat only enough to combine all the ingredients to a smooth and creamy batter.

♡ When spooning the batter into the paper liners, be careful not to overfill them. They should be about two-thirds full. Use a tablespoon and slide the batter off the spoon into each liner with your little finger or another spoon. To fill miniature paper liners, use a teaspoon.

♡ Once the cakes are in the oven, don't be tempted to take a peek too soon. Opening the oven door will let cold air rush in, which will make the cakes sink in the middle.

♡ To check if the cakes are ready, press the tops gently with your fingertip—the cakes should feel just firm and spring back without leaving an indentation.

♡ Once baked, let the cupcakes cool in the muffin pan for 5–10 minutes to let them firm up a little. If you try to move them too quickly, they will crumble. Let the cupcakes cool completely before frosting or decorating.

♡ It almost goes without saying that a cupcake is best eaten on the day of making. However, you can store undecorated cupcakes in an airtight container for 2–3 days. Depending on the topping, decorated cupcakes will keep for 1–2 days in an airtight container. It's best not to store cupcakes in the refrigerator unless they have a chocolate or cream-base topping. Remove from the refrigerator at least 30 minutes before serving. Plain and buttercream-topped cupcakes can be frozen for up to 1 month.

What went wrong?

Overpeaked—too much leavening agent or oven temperature too hot.

Dip in the center—not cooked for long enough and/or oven door opened too soon.

Dense and heavy texture—insufficient creaming or too heavy-handed when folding in.

Basic Vanilla Cupcakes

Follow these 10 simple steps for success every time.

MAKES 12

½ cup butter, softened, or soft margarine

generous ½ cup superfine sugar

2 eggs, lightly beaten

1 tsp vanilla extract

scant 1 cup self-rising flour

1 tbsp milk

Step 1

Preheat the oven to 350°F/ 180°C. Put 12 paper liners in a shallow muffin pan.

Step 2

Put the butter and sugar into a large bowl. Using a wooden spoon or an electric mixer, beat together until the batter is pale, light, and fluffy.

Step 3

Gradually beat in the eggs. Add about 1 tablespoonful at a time and beat thoroughly after each addition.

Step 4

Beat in the vanilla extract. Using a large metal strainer or a sifter, sift the flour into the bowl.

Step 5

Using a metal spoon, gently fold the flour into the batter until thoroughly incorporated.

Step 6

Add the milk and fold gently into the batter.

Step 7

The cupcake batter should have a smooth consistency and drop easily from the spoon if tapped on the side of the bowl.

Step 8

Carefully spoon the batter into the paper liners, being careful not to overfill them.

Step 9

Bake in the preheated oven for 15–20 minutes, or until the cupcakes are risen, golden, and just firm to the touch.

Step 10

Let the cupcakes cool in the pan for about 10 minutes, then carefully transfer to a wire rack. Let cool completely.

Flavor variations

Lemon or orange—add the finely grated rind of 1 small lemon or orange to the butter and sugar in step 2.

Chocolate—replace 2 tablespoons of the self-rising flour with unsweetened cocoa.

Coffee—replace the milk with 1 tablespoon of cold strong black coffee.

Almond—replace the vanilla extract with 1 teaspoon of almond extract.

Peppermint—replace the vanilla extract with 1 teaspoon of peppermint extract.

Vanilla Buttercream

Smooth and buttery, vanilla-flavored buttercream is the ideal topping for cupcakes. It's simple to make, is easy to spread or pipe, and tastes delicious!

TOPS 12 CUPCAKES

scant ¾ cup unsalted butter, softened

1 tsp vanilla extract

2¼ cups confectioners' sugar

1–2 tbsp milk

Step 1

Place the butter and vanilla extract in a large mixing bowl and, using an electric mixer, beat the butter until very soft and pale.

Step 2

Gradually sift in the confectioners' sugar, beating well after each addition. The more you beat at this stage, the lighter and fluffier the frosting will be. Beat in the milk to produce a softer consistency for piping.

☆ If not using right away, transfer the buttercream to a small bowl and cover with plastic wrap. It will keep in a cool place for 2–3 days. Stored in the refrigerator, buttercream will keep for up to a week but will become very firm, so let it stand at room temperature for at least 1 hour before using.

☆ To color, use a toothpick to add a tiny amount of food coloring paste or liquid to the buttercream. Beat thoroughly until you have an even color.

Flavor variations

Chocolate—beat in 2 tablespoons of unsweetened cocoa mixed to a paste with a little hot water, or 4 oz/115 g melted milk or semisweet chocolate.

Lemon or orange—beat in the finely grated rind and juice of 1 large lemon or orange and omit the milk.

Coffee—replace the milk with 1–2 tablespoons of cold strong black coffee or 1 tablespoon of coffee extract.

Caramel—beat in 1–2 tablespoons of dulce de leche (caramel sauce).

Frosting Cupcakes by Hand

The simplest way to top cupcakes with buttercream is to spread or swirl the frosting with a palette knife. Here's a quick guide to a variety of different finishes.

First, make sure that the buttercream is as smooth and creamy as possible, with no small lumps, by beating thoroughly with a spatula.

For a simple lightly swirled topping, take a good scoop of buttercream on the palette knife and place it on the top of the cupcake. Spread the frosting to the edges of the cupcake and, using a back-and-forth motion and without lifting the knife from the frosting, spread the buttercream evenly over the cake.

To create a smooth domed effect, perfect for coating with sugar sprinkles, add more buttercream to the center of the cupcake. Use the palette knife to smooth the frosting right down to the edge of the cupcake liner, then lightly smooth the top.

To achieve a raised edge effect, add a little more buttercream and spread it out to the edges of the cupcake, leaving a small dip in the middle. Holding the palette knife at an angle to the side of the cupcake, drag it all around the cupcake to produce a smooth raised edge of frosting.

For a really generously topped cupcake with big swirls of frosting, add another scoop of buttercream to the top of the cupcake. Drag the end of the knife through the frosting in the center of the cupcake in a circular motion to create a deep swirl. Without lifting the knife from the frosting, drag it back in the opposite direction, then quickly lift the knife away.

Piping Buttercream

Piping buttercream onto cupcakes gives a professional finish and is surprisingly easy.

♡ **To fill a pastry bag with frosting,** use a large pastry bag fitted with a star or plain tip. Hold the pastry bag in one hand with the top of the bag folded down over your fingers and thumb. Use a spatula to scoop the frosting into the bag. Unfold the top of the bag, then gently smooth the frosting down into the bag to remove any pockets of air. Twist the bag tightly at the top to prevent the frosting from being squeezed up and out of the bag.

Alternatively, you can place the pastry bag in a tall glass and fold the top of the bag over the rim of the glass. This will leave you with both hands free to fill the bag with frosting.

♡ **To pipe swirls of frosting,** use a pastry bag fitted with a large star tip and position the tip near the outer edge of the top of the cupcake. Squeeze the pastry bag firmly and, as the frosting comes out of the nozzle, gently rotate the pastry bag in a decreasing circle toward the center of the cake. Once the top of the cupcake is covered, stop squeezing the bag and lift the tip gently away from the cupcake to create a pointed peak of frosting in the center.

♡ **For large swirls of frosting,** pipe two or three decreasing circles of frosting on top of the cupcake, gently lifting the bag as you work.

♡ **To pipe rose swirls of frosting,** use a medium-size star tip and start piping from the center of the cupcake. Keep the nozzle close to the top of the cupcake and continue piping in a spiral pattern until the cake is covered.

Filling a pastry bag

Ready to pipe

Swirls of frosting

Rose swirls

Glace Icing

You can make a glace icing from confectioners' sugar and water. It gives a wonderful smooth finish to cupcakes and sets softly in about 30 minutes. It's easy to flavor and color and can be used to create pretty feathering or fanning effects or can be simply drizzled over cupcakes.

TOPS 12 CUPCAKES

generous 1⅓ cups confectioners' sugar

5–6 tsp warm water

Step 1

Sift the confectioners' sugar into a bowl. Add 2 teaspoons of the water and beat well with a wooden spoon.

Step 2

Continue adding the water a little at a time until you have a smooth and thick icing that will coat the back of the wooden spoon.

☆Use immediately or cover the surface of the icing with plastic wrap and use within 1 hour. Stir thoroughly before using and, if the icing has thickened a little, beat in a few drops of hot water.

☆To color the icing, add a few drops of liquid food coloring or a very tiny amount of paste coloring on the tip of a toothpick and stir until thoroughly mixed.

Flavor variations

Lemon or orange—replace the water with lemon juice or orange juice and add a little finely grated rind, if liked.

Coffee—replace the water with coffee extract or cold strong black coffee.

Chocolate—replace 3 tablespoons of the confectioners' sugar with unsweetened cocoa.

Almond or vanilla—replace ½ teaspoon of the water with ½ teaspoon of almond extract or vanilla extract.

To feather cupcake icing, spoon the icing over the top of the cupcakes to cover completely. Spoon a contrasting colored or flavored icing into a pastry bag fitted with a fine tip and quickly pipe parallel lines across the top. Use a toothpick to draw lightly across the piped lines in alternate directions to create a feathered effect.

Feather & Fan

To fan cupcake icing, instead of piping lines of contrasting icing, pipe three or four concentric circles. Create a fanned or spiderweb effect by alternately drawing a toothpick through the icing from the center of the cupcake to the edge and from the edge back to the center.

Royal Icing

Royal icing is a smooth, fluid icing made from egg white and confectioners' sugar. It's perfect for piping intricate decorations because it holds its shape well and sets hard. It's also useful for attaching decorations to fondant or for making pretty run-out designs to decorate cupcakes.

MAKES ABOUT 1¼ CUPS

2 tbsp egg white

1¼ cups confectioners' sugar, sifted

a few drops of lemon juice (optional)

Step 1

Place the egg white in a bowl and, using a fork, whisk until just frothy.

Step 2

Using an electric mixer or wooden spoon, gradually beat in the confectioners' sugar until the batter is stiff and stands up in peaks when the beaters or spoon are lifted. To produce the desired consistency for piping, beat in a few drops of lemon juice, if using.

♡ A few drops of edible glycerin (from a cake supplier) added with the lemon juice will stop the icing from setting too hard.

♡ Once made, royal icing will keep for a few days, as long as the surface is closely covered with plastic wrap. Beat thoroughly before using and add a few drops of warm water to loosen the icing, if necessary.

♡ Royal icing is best colored with food coloring pastes, because liquids will affect the piping consistency. Add coloring paste sparingly with a toothpick and beat well.

Chocolate Ganache

Chocolate ganache is the ultimate chocolate topping for cupcakes. Made from good-quality dark chocolate and heavy cream, it has a beautifully glossy sheen and is ideal for piping in large swirls on top of cupcakes.

TOPS 12 CUPCAKES

5½ oz/150 g semisweet chocolate

scant 1 cup heavy cream

Step 1

Finely chop the chocolate and place in a heatproof bowl. Heat the cream in a small saucepan until almost at boiling point. Pour the cream over the chocolate.

Step 2

Stir until the chocolate has melted and the batter is smooth.

♡ For a pouring glaze to cover the tops of cupcakes, use the ganache immediately.

♡ For spreading, let the ganache cool for 15–20 minutes, stirring occasionally, until thickened.

♡ For a firmer piping consistency, let the ganache cool for 5 minutes, then beat with an electric mixer until it has cooled and thickened and is the consistency of softened butter.

♡ To make small truffles to decorate cupcakes, chill the cooled ganache until firm. Roll into tiny balls and dust with unsweetened cocoa or confectioners' sugar.

Piping Techniques & Tips

Whether it's big bold swirls of frosting or delicate designs in royal icing, piping turns a simple cupcake into something special.

♡ Piping tips

For piping buttercream, whipped cream, or cream cheese frostings, you will need large, plain or star tips made of metal or plastic. Wide tips will let the frosting come out more quickly and produce big swirls.

For piping a simple icing or royal icing, use small, fine metal tips. You'll need one with a plain tip for piping fine lines, dots, lettering, and lacy patterns, and a star-shaped tip for piping shells, stars, and rope patterns.

♡ Pastry bags

Whether you choose to use reusable or disposable pastry bags, make sure to suit the size of the bag to the quantity of frosting or icing you are using.

For piping cream, meringue, buttercream, and other frostings, use large bags that have plenty of room for filling. Don't overfill the bag—you need to leave enough space at the top to twist it tightly closed to contain the frosting.

For a simple icing or royal icing, use a small or medium bag. Disposable or paper pastry bags are handy if you have several different-colored icings to work with at one time.

Making a paper pastry bag

Cut a 10-inch/25-cm square of wax paper, fold it diagonally in half, and cut into two triangles. Take one triangle and hold the two points at each end of the long edge. Curl one point over to meet the center point, making a cone shape, then curl the other point over so all three points meet. Fold the points over a few times to secure the cone. Snip off the end and use with or without a tip.

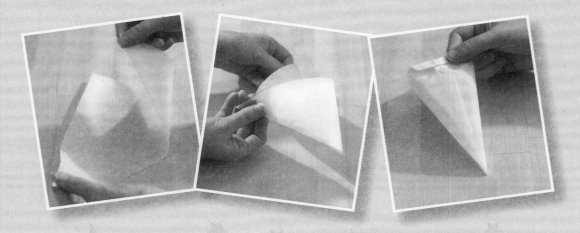

Piping simple icing or royal icing

Lines and lettering—use a small bag with a fine writing tip. Place the tip on the surface to be iced and squeeze the bag gently. As the icing comes out of the tip, lift the bag so the icing falls in a straight line or curve on the surface. To finish piping, stop squeezing and gently press the tip on the surface to end the line of icing neatly.

Cornelli/lace effect—use a small bag with a fine writing tip. Starting at an outer edge, pipe a random meandering line of icing all over the surface of the cupcake. Try not to let the lines touch or cross and keep even pressure on the pastry bag so the lines are of the same thickness.

Store-Bought Decorations

✩ **Sugar sprinkles**—probably the simplest and easiest way to give frosted or iced cupcakes a touch of colorful fun, sugar sprinkles are readily available in a huge variety of colors, shapes, and sizes. From the classic strands to small shimmering pearls, pastel-colored flower shapes, or tiny red hearts, there's a sprinkle to suit any occasion! Always add sprinkles before the icing or frosting has set, otherwise they will drop off.

✩ **Sanding sugar**—this is a coarse sugar, with grains about four times larger than granulated sugar, that won't dissolve. You can buy it in a range of pastel or vibrant colors. Sanding sugar adds a stylish sparkle when sprinkled over iced cupcakes.

✩ **Edible glitter**—available in tiny jars from cake-decorating suppliers, a little edible glitter can really add the finishing touch to cupcakes for special occasions. Lightly sprinkle over an iced cupcake or use a fine paintbrush to brush onto fondant or piped decorations. Use sparingly.

✩ **Candies and chocolates**—small candies and chocolates are great for jazzing up frosted cupcakes. Candy-covered chocolates, chocolate disks, jelly beans, and gummi bears are all ideal for children's party cupcakes and a sprinkling of popping candy just before serving will make them extra special!

☆ **Sugar flowers and shapes**—simple sugar flowers, animal faces, or themed seasonal shapes are ideal to have in the pantry for last-minute decorations.

☆ **Fresh fruit**—for a refreshing and delicious alternative to sweet sugary sprinkles, use fresh fruit to decorate cupcakes. Try grapes, small berries, or slices of mango, pineapple, peach, or apricot. Arrange on the frosting or icing just before serving and eat on the day of topping.

☆ **Candied rose petals or violets**—delicately perfumed and with a crisp sugary coating, a single deep pink rose petal or purple violet will look stunning on top of a simply iced cupcake, adding a touch of class.

☆ **Nuts**—finely chopped, toasted, whole, halved, or slivered, nuts are a quick and easy way to decorate a cupcake and can complement a flavoring or frosting. To lightly toast nuts, spread on a baking sheet and place in a hot oven for a few minutes until light golden, or put under a hot broiler. Always store nuts in a cool dry place and check the expiration date, because they can turn rancid if kept for too long.

The cherry on the cake

☆**Coconut**—dry unsweetened, flaked or shredded coconut is another quick and effective decoration for cupcakes. Use lightly toasted for an extra-nutty flavor.

☆**Dragées**—these tiny and shiny edible balls are classic cupcake decorations. They are available in a variety of shimmering colors, including silver, gold, pink, blue, and green. You can also buy large silver balls or heart-shaped dragées.

☆**Fresh flowers and herbs**—for a lovely summery decoration, try topping cupcakes with fresh flowers. Make absolutely sure that the flower is edible and wash carefully in cold water, then let dry on paper towels in a cool place before using. Place either the whole flower or a few petals on the cupcake just before serving. Herbs, such as mint and lemon balm, also make pretty decorations, especially when used with fresh or sugar-frosted fruit.

☆**Candied citrus peel**—with a firm and slightly grainy texture, candied lemon, orange, or citron peel can be chopped or cut into thin strips to decorate iced cupcakes. For a more striking decoration, dip very thin strips of peel in melted semisweet chocolate and let set on a wire rack to cool, then arrange a few strips on each cupcake.

☆**Nonedible decorations**—candles and indoor sparklers make great last-minute decorations, especially for birthday or special-occasion cupcakes. Small plastic figurines or shapes can also be used to suit an event, but do remind everyone they are not edible and must be removed before eating the cupcake.

Decorating with Chocolate

Chocolate is perfect for making simple or elaborate decorations to adorn cupcakes.

♡ Melting chocolate ♡

Break the chocolate into pieces and place in a large heatproof bowl. Set the bowl over a saucepan of simmering water, making sure the bowl does not touch the water, and let stand until the chocolate has melted. Remove the bowl from the pan and stir the chocolate until smooth.

Be careful not to let any drips of condensation come into contact with the melting chocolate or it will become grainy and "seize" into solid lumps. For the same reason, if a recipe calls for melting chocolate with a liquid, such as milk, cream, or alcohol, add the liquid to the bowl before you start the melting process.

To melt chocolate in the microwave, break the pieces into a bowl and microwave on a medium setting for 1–2 minutes at a time, until almost completely melted. Remove from the microwave and let stand for 2 minutes, then stir until smooth. If there are any lumps remaining, microwave for another 30 seconds–1 minute.

♡ Making chocolate caraque ♡

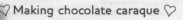

Spread melted semisweet, milk, or white chocolate in a thin and even layer onto a flat marble slab or a clean smooth surface. Let stand until just set but not completely solid. Drag a thin-blade sharp knife across the surface of the chocolate to scrape away long or short curls.

If the chocolate breaks rather than curls, it is too cold. If it sticks to the knife, it has not set enough.

♡ Making simple chocolate curls or shavings ♡

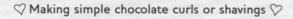

Leave a chunky bar of chocolate at room temperature for at least an hour to soften a little. Run a swivel-blade vegetable peeler along the side of the bar of chocolate to shave off small curls or fine shavings.

♡ Making chocolate leaves ♡

Fresh leaves with well-defined veins, such as bay, rose, mint, and holly, are best to use. Make sure they are thoroughly clean and dry. Brush the underside of each leaf thickly with melted chocolate, being careful not to let the chocolate go over the edges of the leaves. If you are using holly leaves, don't let the chocolate drip over the prickly points. Place the leaves chocolate-side up on a sheet of parchment paper and let stand in a cool place until set. Carefully peel away the leaves from the chocolate. It's worth making more leaves than you need because they are fragile.

♡ Making piped chocolate shapes ♡

Line a baking sheet with parchment paper. Spoon melted chocolate into a paper pastry bag and snip off the very end tip of the bag. Pipe simple shapes, such as flowers, swirls, or motifs, onto the paper. Don't make them too intricate or they will be too fragile. Let stand in a cool place until set, then carefully peel the paper away from the chocolate. Use a small palette knife to move the shapes because the warmth of your fingers will melt the finely piped chocolate.

Decorating with Fondant

Fondant (also known as sugar paste) is a soft and pliable icing that is available from specialty cake suppliers and online. You'll find containers of ready-to-use white or ivory fondant as well as colored versions.

Coloring fondant

It's best to use a food coloring paste to color fondant because liquid will make it sticky. First, knead the fondant until smooth. Smear a little food coloring from the end of a toothpick onto the fondant, then knead the fondant until you have an even color. Add a little more coloring until you get the desired depth of color. Wrap the fondant tightly in plastic wrap to prevent it from drying out.

To marble fondant, knead two different colors of fondant lightly together. To achieve the best effect, use about one third of a deeply colored fondant and two thirds of much paler color or white fondant and be careful not to overknead.

Rolling out fondant

Lightly dust a clean work surface with confectioners' sugar and knead the fondant until smooth. Using a small rolling pin (a nonstick one is best), roll out thinly, lifting and turning the fondant occasionally to prevent it from sticking.

Cutting out shapes

To top cupcakes with a round of fondant, use a round or fluted cookie cutter roughly the size of the top of the cupcake. Stamp the cutter firmly onto the rolled-out fondant, twisting it slightly. Brush or spread a little jelly, chocolate spread, simple icing, or royal icing on the top of the cupcake. Lift the round of fondant with a palette knife and gently place on top of the cupcake.

For small shapes, such as stars, hearts, letters, numbers, and flowers, roll out a small amount of fondant. Stamp out the required shapes and carefully lift with a small angled palette knife. To attach the shapes to fondant-topped cupcakes, use a dab of water, or simple icing or royal icing to stick them into place.

To dry small shapes for decoration, place on a sheet of parchment paper and let stand in a cool place for at least 24 hours. Once firm, they can be placed at angles on top of frosted cupcakes.

Fun with shapes !

Molding shapes

Using small pieces of fondant, you can mold simple shapes to decorate cupcakes. Lightly dust your hands with confectioners' sugar to prevent the fondant from sticking to them.

Decorating with Marzipan

This pliable almond paste can be used in the same way as fondant to decorate cupcakes, but it has a slightly moister texture, which makes it more difficult to color and roll out thinly.

When coloring marzipan, use the white variety and be careful not to add too much coloring because it will become sticky.

Making marzipan or fondant flowers

Roll six or seven pea-size pieces of marzipan or fondant in the palm of your hand into balls.

Place the balls between two sheets of plastic wrap and flatten with a small rolling pin to make petal shapes.

Place a marble-size piece of marzipan or fondant on a small board and shape into a pointed cone for the bottom of the rose.

Take one of the petals and gently wrap around the cone base to form a bud.

Continue wrapping the petals around the bud to create a rose, gently squeezing the bottom of the rose to make the petals curl out.

Use a sharp knife to cut the rose away from the base and let dry in a cool place.

To dust the edges with edible glitter, use a fine paintbrush to lightly brush the tops of the petals with a little water. Dip into edible glitter, then gently tap the roses on a sheet of paper towel to remove any excess glitter. Let stand in a cool place until dry.

Pretty as a picture

Sugar Frosting Fruit, Flowers & Herbs

Choose firm berries, such as blueberries, raspberries, red currants, and strawberries, or small grapes. Make sure that they have no blemishes or soft patches.

Flowers or single petals should be clean and edible (see below). Rose petals work especially well.

Leafy herbs, such as mint, lemon balm, and bay, are ideal for sugar frosting, or try small sprigs of fresh thyme or marjoram.

Using a small paintbrush, lightly brush the fruit, flowers, petals, or leaves all over with a little beaten egg white, making sure to coat the underside of leaves and petals.

Coat flowers with sugar by holding over a plate and sprinkling liberally with superfine sugar, shaking off any excess sugar. To coat leaves, petals, and berries, place the sugar on a flat plate and either dip or roll in the sugar to coat.

Place on a sheet of parchment paper or a wire rack and let stand in cool place for a few hours or overnight until dry. Berries will only keep for a day, but grapes, leaves, and flowers will keep for 2–3 days stored in a cool dry place.

 Edible flowers

Roses Lavender

Marigolds Pansies

Nasturtiums

Building Cupcake Shapes

By stacking different-size cupcakes on top of each other you can create large, fun novelty cupcakes, such as the Ghostly Ghoul Cupcakes (see page 212). You can also build up three-dimensional shapes with mini doughnuts, marshmallows, ice-cream cones, or rolled balls of fondant or marzipan.

To make sure the stacked shapes stick together, spread with plenty of buttercream or icing. Chill the assembled cupcakes until the icing is firm before covering in fondant or frosting.

More ideas for shaped cupcakes

Christmas trees—follow the same stacking method as for the Ghostly Ghoul Cupcakes, but shape the balls of fondant into triangular points to resemble the tops of the trees. Spread or pipe all over with green-colored buttercream and dot with silver dragées.

Witches' hats—spread a raised mound of green buttercream over the top of each cupcake. Place a small inverted waffle ice-cream cone on top of each to resemble a witch's hat. Use tubes of writing icing to pipe eyes, a nose, and straggly black hair under the hat.

Beehives—top each cupcake with another upturned cupcake. Using a large plain piping tip, pipe lines of honey-flavored buttercream all around the raised cupcakes to create a beehive effect. Decorate with fondant bees and flowers.

Making your Cupcakes Special

Edging and coating cupcakes

A simple way to give frosted cupcakes a colorful or decorative finish is to coat the top or edges lightly with sugar sprinkles, grated chocolate, finely chopped nuts, colored sugar, or crushed boiled candies.

To edge cupcakes, spread the coating on a flat plate. Hold a cupcake by its bottom and quickly roll the raised frosted edge in the coating, shaking off any excess.

To completely coat cupcakes, smooth the frosting over the cupcake in a raised mound. Hold the cupcake over a plate and liberally sprinkle with the coating, pressing down lightly with your fingers, if necessary.

When using buttercream, it's best to frost and coat the cupcakes one at a time, otherwise the frosting will dry a little and the coating will not stick.

Stenciling designs on cupcakes

Simple but very effective designs can be created for the top of cupcakes using store-bought or homemade stencils and dusting with unsweetened cocoa, confectioners' sugar, colored sugar, or finely grated chocolate.

Small coffee stencils with simple designs, such as hearts, flowers, and stars, are ideal to use. Hold steadily close to the surface of the cupcake and liberally spoon or shake over sifted unsweetened cocoa, confectioners' sugar, colored sugar, or sprinkles. Gently lift away the stencil.

Alternatively, cut out your own simple shapes from a piece of cardboard, or, to create a lacy pattern, cut a round piece of a paper doily to fit the top of the cupcake.

For a geometric design, lay thin strips of paper gently on top of the cupcake and dust liberally with confectioners' sugar or unsweetened cocoa. Carefully lift away the strips of paper.

Adding flavor to cupcakes

Brushing or spooning syrup over cupcakes while they are still warm from the oven will infuse them with extra flavor, as well as helping to keep them deliciously moist. This is especially useful when making a big batch of cupcakes for a special event.

To make a basic sugar syrup, place a generous 3 tablespoons of superfine sugar and 4 tablespoons of water in a small saucepan and heat gently until the sugar dissolves. Boil, without stirring, for about 1 minute, until syrupy, then let cool for at least 10 minutes.

Use a skewer to pierce a few holes in the top of the warm cupcakes and liberally spoon or brush the syrup over the top. Let cool completely before topping with frosting or icing.

Syrup flavors

Lemon or orange—replace the water with lemon juice or orange juice.

Coffee—add 2 teaspoons of instant coffee powder.

Rum—replace 2 tablespoons of the water with dark rum.

Vanilla or almond—add 1 teaspoon of vanilla extract or almond extract.

Hidden fillings for cupcakes

To add a surprise element to cupcakes, try scooping out a little of the cake and adding a sweet filling.

Suit the filling to the flavor of the cupcake. Strawberry or raspberry jelly goes particularly well with vanilla or almond cupcakes. Try chocolate hazelnut spread with chocolate or coffee cupcakes, and lemon curd with citrus-flavored cupcakes.

To scoop out the cake, make sure the cupcake is completely cold, then use a teaspoon or the tip of a small knife to cut away a small piece of cake. Spoon a little of the filling into the hole, being careful not to overfill, and then place the piece of cake back in place, pressing down gently.

The Finishing Touches

When serving cupcakes on special occasions or giving them as gifts, it's well worth taking a little time to think about the presentation or packaging. From traditional cake stands to beautiful boxes and colorful ribbons, the finishing touches make all the difference!

Cupcake banners

A quick and easy way to jazz up cupcakes for a party or special event is to decorate them with small banners. You can buy these already made, often themed for seasonal events, such as Christmas or Halloween, or make your own to suit the occasion.

To make your own, cut out a small piece of thin cardboard or paper (plain or patterned) using the template on this page as a guide. Fold around a toothpick and glue together the two halves. If liked, draw a simple design on the banners or write a message on them.

To make heart-shaped or flower-shaped cupcake banners, trace the outline of a small cookie cutter onto colored cardboard. Cut out carefully and, using glue or double-sided tape, attach two identical shapes back-to-back on a toothpick.

Template

Gift tags

A box of cupcakes given as a gift for a special occasion needs labeling with a pretty gift or name tag.

Gift tags are available to buy in a range of colors and sizes and you can pick them to suit the color or flavor of cupcake being given. However, for a more personal touch why not make your own?

To make your own, choose a piece of firm paper or thin cardboard and use one of the templates on this page as a guide to cut out the gift tag shape. Make a hole at the end or corner of the tag with a hole puncher and thread with thin ribbon or string.

Templates

Perfect Presentation

Whether you've just got friends over for a coffee or you're celebrating a more formal occasion, such as a birthday or wedding, always make your homemade cupcakes center stage by arranging them on pretty plates or stands.

Cake plates—elegantly decorated cupcakes look even more delicious when arranged on pretty ceramic plates or cake stands. Make sure that you don't position the cupcakes too close together—allow enough room so that you can take a cake from the plate or stand without damaging any of the others. Add extra decorations around the cupcakes, if liked, such as small flowers, fresh herbs, sugared almonds, ribbons, or small bows.

Cupcake stands—these are ideal for displaying and serving batches of cupcakes. Special metal stands with individual wired holders for each cupcake, which ensure that the frosting or icing doesn't get damaged, are ideal. Alternatively, look out for cheaper disposable cardboard stands in a variety of colors and patterns. Both types can hold 20–30 cupcakes—enough for a party or small wedding. For a larger quantity of cupcakes, it may be worth renting a tiered cake stand from a specialty cake supplier or make your own tiered stand using different-size cake boards and cake pillars.

Cupcake wrappers—these decorative strips of light cardboard come in a variety of patterns and colors and are great for wrapping around individual cupcakes. Some have themed designs, while others have fancy laced or scalloped edges. They are simply wrapped around single cupcakes and sealed with a tab fastening.

Gift boxes—available in a huge range of sizes and colors, gift boxes are an ideal way to give cupcakes as presents. Look for boxes with a clear panel in the top so that you can see the contents without opening the lid. Some kitchen stores stock cupcake boxes with special inserts, into which you can slot the cupcakes to hold them safely in place.

Cellophane bags—these are the perfect way to present a single cupcake as a gift. They are available in clear or patterned versions. Tie them with a pretty ribbon for an extra-special touch.

Summer Garden Cupcakes

MAKES 8

½ cup butter, softened, or soft margarine

generous ½ cup superfine sugar

2 tsp rose water

2 extra large eggs, lightly beaten

scant 1 cup self-rising flour

TO DECORATE

4 oz/115 g pink ready-to-use fondant

confectioners' sugar, for dusting

3 oz/85 g white ready-to-use fondant

3 oz/85 g blue ready-to-use fondant

tube of yellow writing icing

BUTTERCREAM

¾ cup unsalted butter, softened

6 tbsp heavy cream

2¾ cups confectioners' sugar

green food coloring

Preheat the oven to 350°F/180°C. Put 8 paper liners into a shallow muffin pan.

Place the butter, superfine sugar, and rose water in a large bowl and beat together until light and fluffy. Gradually beat in the eggs. Sift in the flour and, using a metal spoon, fold in gently.

Spoon the batter into the paper liners. Bake in the preheated oven for 15–20 minutes, or until risen, golden, and firm to the touch. Transfer to a wire rack and let cool.

Roll out the pink fondant to a thickness of ¼ inch/5 mm on a surface lightly dusted with confectioners' sugar. Using a small butterfly cutter, stamp out 16 butterflies. Roll out the white and blue fondants to the same thickness and, using a small daisy cutter, stamp out about 40 flowers, rerolling the fondant as necessary. Use the yellow writing icing to pipe centers in the flowers.

To make the buttercream, place the butter in a bowl and beat with an electric mixer for 2–3 minutes, until pale and creamy. Beat in the cream, then gradually sift in the confectioners' sugar and continue beating for 2–3 minutes, until the buttercream is light and fluffy. Beat in a little green food coloring to give a light green color.

Spoon the buttercream into a large pastry bag fitted with a large star tip. Pipe swirls of buttercream on top of each cupcake. Decorate with the fondant butterflies and flowers.

Rocky Road Cupcakes

MAKES 12

2 tbsp unsweetened cocoa

2 tbsp hot water

½ cup butter, softened,
or soft margarine

generous ½ cup superfine
sugar

2 eggs, lightly beaten

scant 1 cup self-rising
flour

TOPPING

¼ cup chopped mixed nuts

3½ oz/100 g milk
chocolate, melted

2 cups miniature
marshmallows

¼ cup chopped candied
cherries

Preheat the oven to 350°F/180°C. Put 12 paper liners into a muffin pan.

Blend the cocoa and hot water and set aside. Place the butter and superfine sugar in a large bowl and beat together until light and fluffy. Gradually beat in the eggs, then beat in the cocoa batter. Sift in the flour and, using a metal spoon, fold in gently.

Spoon the batter into the paper liners. Bake in the preheated oven for 20 minutes, or until risen and firm to the touch. Transfer to a wire rack and let cool.

To make the topping, stir the nuts into the melted chocolate and spread a little of the batter over the top of the cupcakes. Lightly stir the marshmallows and candied cherries into the remaining chocolate batter and pile on top of the cupcakes. Let set.

Ice-Cream Cone Cupcakes

MAKES 8

¾ cup butter, softened, or soft margarine

generous ¾ cup superfine sugar

3 eggs, lightly beaten

1 tsp vanilla extract

1¼ cups self-rising flour

½ cup ground almonds

BUTTERCREAM

1 cup unsalted butter, softened

1 tbsp cream or milk

2¾ cups confectioners' sugar

TO DECORATE

12 miniature chocolate bars

sugar sprinkles

Preheat the oven to 350°F/180°C. Put 8 paper liners into a muffin pan.

Place the butter and superfine sugar in a large bowl and beat together until light and fluffy. Gradually beat in the eggs and vanilla extract. Sift in the flour and, using a metal spoon, fold gently into the batter with the ground almonds.

Spoon the batter into the paper liners. Bake in the preheated oven for 20–25 minutes, or until risen, golden, and firm to the touch. Transfer to a wire rack and let cool.

To make the buttercream, place the butter in a bowl and beat with an electric mixer for 2–3 minutes, until pale and creamy. Beat in the cream, then gradually sift in the confectioners' sugar and continue beating for 2–3 minutes, until the buttercream is light and fluffy.

Spoon the buttercream into a large pastry bag fitted with a large star tip. Pipe swirls of buttercream on top of each cupcake to resemble ice cream. Press a chocolate bar into each swirl of buttercream and scatter with sugar sprinkles.

Lollipop Cupcakes

MAKES 12

½ cup butter, softened, or soft margarine

generous ½ cup superfine sugar

2 tsp finely grated orange rind

2 eggs, lightly beaten

scant 1 cup self-rising flour

BUTTERCREAM

½ cup unsalted butter, softened

2 tbsp orange juice

1¾ cups confectioners' sugar

orange food coloring

TO DECORATE

3 oz/85 g green ready-to-use fondant

confectioners' sugar, for dusting

red sugar sprinkles

12 small candy lollipops

Preheat the oven to 350°F/180°C. Put 12 paper liners into a shallow muffin pan.

Place the butter, superfine sugar, and orange rind in a large bowl and beat together until light and fluffy. Gradually beat in the eggs. Sift in the flour and, using a metal spoon, fold in gently.

Spoon the batter into the paper liners. Bake in the preheated oven for 15–20 minutes, or until risen, golden, and firm to the touch. Transfer to a wire rack and let cool.

To make the buttercream, place the butter and orange juice in a bowl and beat with an electric mixer for 2–3 minutes, until pale and creamy. Gradually sift in the confectioners' sugar and continue beating for 2–3 minutes, until the buttercream is light and fluffy. Beat in a little orange food coloring.

Roll out the green fondant to a thickness of ¼ inch/ 5 mm on a surface lightly dusted with confectioners' sugar. Using a small leaf cutter, stamp out 24 leaves. Swirl the buttercream on the top of the cupcakes and edge with sugar sprinkles. Place a lollipop and 2 fondant leaves in the center of each cupcake.

Chocolate Florentine Cupcakes

MAKES 12

2 oz/55 g semisweet chocolate

6 tbsp butter, softened, or soft margarine

1 tbsp light corn syrup

¼ cup light brown sugar

scant 1 cup self-rising flour

1 extra large egg, lightly beaten

TOPPING

¼ cup chopped candied cherries

¼ cup slivered almonds

1 tbsp raisins

1 tbsp light corn syrup

Preheat the oven to 375°F/190°C. Put 12 paper liners into a shallow muffin pan.

Put the chocolate, butter, corn syrup, and brown sugar in a saucepan and heat gently, stirring occasionally, until just melted. Let cool for 2 minutes.

Sift the flour into a large bowl and pour in the chocolate batter. Add the egg and beat until thoroughly blended.

Spoon the batter into the paper liners. Mix the topping ingredients together and gently spoon a little of the batter on top of each cupcake.

Bake in the preheated oven for 15–20 minutes, or until risen and firm to the touch. Transfer to a wire rack and let cool.

Strawberries & Cream Cupcakes

MAKES 10

6 tbsp butter, softened, or soft margarine

scant ½ cup superfine sugar

1 extra large egg, lightly beaten

½ tsp vanilla extract

⅔ cup self-rising flour

1 tbsp milk

⅓ cup raisins

TO DECORATE

⅔ cup hulled and sliced small strawberries

1 tbsp strawberry jelly

½ cup whipped heavy cream

confectioners' sugar, for dusting

Preheat the oven to 375°F/190°C. Put 10 paper liners into a shallow muffin pan.

Place the butter and superfine sugar in a large bowl and beat together until light and fluffy. Gradually beat in the egg and vanilla extract. Sift in the flour and, using a metal spoon, fold gently into the batter with the milk and raisins.

Spoon the batter into the paper liners. Bake in the preheated oven for 15–20 minutes, or until risen, golden, and firm to the touch. Transfer to a wire rack and let cool.

Use a serrated knife to cut a circle from the top of each cupcake. Gently mix together the strawberries and jelly and divide among the cupcakes. Top each with a small dollop of whipped cream. Replace the cupcake tops and dust with confectioners' sugar.

Feather-Iced Coffee Cupcakes

MAKES 16

scant 1 cup self-rising flour

½ tsp baking powder

½ cup butter, softened, or soft margarine

½ cup light brown sugar

2 eggs, lightly beaten

1 tbsp instant coffee powder dissolved in 1 tbsp boiling water, cooled

2 tbsp sour cream

ICING

1¾ cups confectioners' sugar

4 tsp warm water

1 tbsp instant coffee powder dissolved in 2 tbsp boiling water

Preheat the oven to 375°F/190°C. Put 16 paper liners into shallow muffin pans.

Sift the flour and baking powder into a large bowl. Add the butter, brown sugar, and eggs and, using an electric mixer, beat together until smooth. Beat in the dissolved coffee and sour cream.

Spoon the batter into the paper liners. Bake in the preheated oven for 20 minutes, or until risen, golden, and firm to the touch. Transfer to a wire rack and let cool.

To make the icing, sift ⅔ cup of the confectioners' sugar into a bowl, then gradually mix in the water. Sift the remaining confectioners' sugar into a separate bowl, then stir in the dissolved coffee.

Spoon the coffee icing into a pastry bag fitted with a fine tip. Spoon the white icing over the cupcakes to cover completely. Quickly pipe parallel lines of the coffee icing across the top. Use a toothpick to draw lightly across the piped lines in alternate directions to create a feathered effect.

Lemon Butterfly Cupcakes

MAKES 12

scant 1 cup self-rising flour

½ tsp baking powder

½ cup butter, softened, or soft margarine

generous ½ cup superfine sugar

2 eggs, lightly beaten

finely grated rind of ½ lemon

2 tbsp milk

BUTTERCREAM

6 tbsp unsalted butter, softened

1⅓ cups confectioners' sugar, plus extra for dusting

1 tbsp lemon juice

Preheat the oven to 375°F/190°C. Put 12 paper liners into a shallow muffin pan.

Sift the flour and baking powder into a large bowl. Add the butter, superfine sugar, eggs, lemon rind, and milk and, using an electric mixer, beat together until smooth.

Spoon the batter into the paper liners. Bake in the preheated oven for 15–20 minutes, or until risen, golden, and firm to the touch. Transfer to a wire rack and let cool.

To make the buttercream, put the butter in a bowl and beat until fluffy. Sift in the confectioners' sugar, add the lemon juice, and beat together until smooth and creamy.

Use a serrated knife to cut a circle from the top of each cupcake, then cut each circle in half. Spread or pipe a little of the buttercream onto the center of each cupcake, then press two semicircular halves into it at an angle to resemble butterfly wings. Dust with confectioners' sugar.

Jelly-Filled Cupcakes

MAKES 28

1⅓ cups all-purpose flour

1 tbsp baking powder

1 tbsp vanilla pudding mix

¾ cup butter, softened, or soft margarine

generous ¾ cup superfine sugar

3 eggs, lightly beaten

1 tsp vanilla extract

¼ cup raspberry jelly

confectioners' sugar, for dusting

Preheat the oven to 375°F/190°C. Put 28 paper liners into shallow muffin pans.

Sift the flour, baking powder, and pudding mix into a large bowl. Add the butter, superfine sugar, eggs, and vanilla extract and, using an electric mixer, beat together until smooth.

Spoon the batter into the paper liners and place ½ teaspoon of the jelly onto the center of each, without pressing down.

Bake in the preheated oven for 15–20 minutes, or until risen, golden, and firm to the touch. Transfer to a wire rack and let cool. Dust with confectioners' sugar.

Ladybug Cupcakes

MAKES 10

scant 1 cup self-rising flour

½ tsp baking powder

½ cup butter, softened, or soft margarine

generous ½ cup superfine sugar

2 extra large eggs, lightly beaten

3 oz/85 g milk chocolate, melted

1 tbsp milk

TO DECORATE

8 oz/225 g red ready-to-use fondant

confectioners' sugar, for dusting

2 tbsp raspberry jelly

3 oz/85 g black ready-to-use fondant

tubes of black and white writing icing

Preheat the oven to 350°F/180°C. Put 10 paper liners into a muffin pan.

Sift the flour and baking powder into a large bowl. Add the butter, superfine sugar, and eggs and, using an electric mixer, beat together until smooth. Beat in the melted chocolate and milk.

Spoon the batter into the paper liners. Bake in the preheated oven for 18–22 minutes, until risen and firm to the touch. Transfer to a wire rack and let cool.

Roll out the red fondant to a thickness of ¼ inch/5 mm on a surface lightly dusted with confectioners' sugar. Using a 2¾-inch/7-cm round cutter, stamp out 10 rounds, rerolling the fondant as necessary. Brush each cupcake lightly with a little of the jelly and gently press a fondant round on top. Roll out the black fondant to the same thickness and cut out 10 ovals for the faces. Lightly brush with water and press on top of the red fondant.

Shape the trimmings from the black fondant into small dots and attach with a dab of water. Use the black writing icing to pipe a line to divide the wings and two small antennae on each cupcake. Use the white writing icing to pipe eyes and a smile onto the face of each ladybug. Dot the eyes with tiny rolled balls of black fondant.

Marbled Chocolate Cupcakes

MAKES 21

generous 1⅓ cups
self-rising flour

¾ cup butter, softened,
or soft margarine

generous ¾ cup superfine
sugar

3 eggs, lightly beaten

2 tbsp milk

2 oz/55 g semisweet
chocolate, melted

Preheat the oven to 350°F/180°C. Put 21 paper liners into shallow muffin pans.

Sift the flour into a large bowl. Add the butter, superfine sugar, eggs, and milk and, using an electric mixer, beat together until smooth.

Divide the batter between two bowls. Add the melted chocolate to one of the bowls and stir until well mixed. Place alternate teaspoonfuls of the two batters into the paper liners.

Bake in the preheated oven for 20 minutes, or until risen and firm to the touch. Transfer to a wire rack and let cool.

Pink & White Cupcakes

MAKES 16

scant 1 cup self-rising flour

1 tsp baking powder

½ cup butter, softened, or soft margarine

generous ½ cup superfine sugar

2 eggs, lightly beaten

1 tbsp milk

red food coloring (optional)

TOPPING

1 egg white

generous ¾ cup superfine sugar

2 tbsp hot water

large pinch of cream of tartar

2 tbsp raspberry jelly

2 tbsp lightly toasted unsweetened dried shredded coconut

Preheat the oven to 350°F/180°C. Put 16 paper liners into shallow muffin pans.

Sift the flour and baking powder into a large bowl. Add the butter, superfine sugar, and eggs and, using an electric mixer, beat together until smooth. Mix the milk with a little red food coloring, if using, and beat into the batter until evenly blended.

Spoon the batter into the paper liners. Bake in the preheated oven for 20 minutes, or until risen, golden, and firm to the touch. Transfer to a wire rack and let cool.

To make the topping, put the egg white, superfine sugar, water, and cream of tartar into a heatproof bowl set over a saucepan of simmering water. Using an electric mixer, beat for 5–6 minutes, until the batter is thick and softly peaks when the beaters are lifted.

Spread a layer of jelly over each cupcake, then swirl over the frosting. Sprinkle with the toasted coconut.

Funny Monkey Cupcakes

MAKES 12

½ cup butter, softened, or soft margarine

scant ½ cup light brown sugar

1 tbsp honey

2 eggs, lightly beaten

¾ cup self-rising flour

2 tbsp unsweetened cocoa

TO DECORATE

12 oz/350 g ivory ready-to-use fondant

brown food coloring

confectioners' sugar, for dusting

2 tbsp chocolate hazelnut spread

24 chocolate disks

tubes of white and black writing icing

12 brown candy-covered chocolate beans

Preheat the oven to 350°F/180°C. Put 12 paper liners into a shallow muffin pan.

Place the butter, brown sugar, and honey in a large bowl and beat together until light and fluffy. Gradually beat in the eggs. Sift in the flour and cocoa and, using a metal spoon, fold in gently.

Spoon the batter into the paper liners. Bake in the preheated oven for 15–20 minutes, until risen and firm to the touch. Transfer to a wire rack and let cool.

Color two-thirds of the ivory fondant pale brown with a little brown food coloring. Roll out the brown fondant to a thickness of ¼ inch/5 mm on a surface lightly dusted with confectioners' sugar. Using a 2¾-inch/7-cm round cutter, stamp out 12 rounds. Roll out the remaining ivory fondant to the same thickness and, using the end of a large plain pastry bag tip, cut out 24 small rounds. Reroll the fondant and cut out 12 ovals.

Spread the top of the cupcakes with a thin layer of chocolate spread and top with the rounds of brown fondant. Attach 2 ivory rounds and 1 oval on top of each cupcake with a little water to resemble a monkey's face. Arrange 2 chocolate disks on the side of each cupcake for ears and attach with some of the writing icing. Use the white and black writing icings to pipe eyes and a mouth and place a chocolate bean in the center of each face for a nose.

Chocolate Cherry Cupcakes

MAKES 12

1 tsp lemon juice

4 tbsp milk

1¼ cups self-rising flour

1 tbsp unsweetened cocoa

½ tsp baking soda

2 eggs, lightly beaten

4 tbsp butter, softened, or soft margarine

generous ½ cup light brown sugar

3 oz/85 g semisweet chocolate, melted

3 tbsp chopped dried and sweetened sour cherries

TO DECORATE

2 tbsp cherry liqueur (optional)

⅔ cup heavy cream, softly whipped

5 tbsp cherry jelly or preserve

unsweetened cocoa, for dusting

Preheat the oven to 350°F/180°C. Put 12 paper liners into a muffin pan.

Add the lemon juice to the milk and let stand for about 10 minutes—the milk will curdle a little.

Sift the flour, unsweetened cocoa, and baking soda into a large bowl. Add the eggs, butter, brown sugar, and milk batter and, using an electric mixer, beat until smooth. Fold in the melted chocolate and sour cherries.

Spoon the batter into the paper liners. Bake in the preheated oven for 20–25 minutes, or until risen and firm to the touch. Transfer to a wire rack and let cool.

Cut a circle from the top of each cupcake. Sprinkle the cupcakes with the cherry liqueur, if using. Spoon the whipped cream onto the centers and top with a small spoonful of jelly. Gently replace the cupcake tops and dust lightly with unsweetened cocoa.

Lemon Meringue Cupcakes

MAKES 4

6 tbsp butter, softened, or soft margarine, plus extra for greasing

scant ½ cup superfine sugar

finely grated rind and juice of ½ lemon

1 extra large egg, lightly beaten

⅔ cup self-rising flour

2 tbsp lemon curd

MERINGUE

2 egg whites

generous ½ cup superfine sugar

Preheat the oven to 375°F/190°C. Grease four 1-cup ramekins or individual baking dishes.

Place the butter, superfine sugar, and lemon rind in a large bowl and beat together until light and fluffy. Gradually beat in the egg. Sift in the flour and, using a metal spoon, fold into the batter with the lemon juice.

Spoon the batter into the ramekins. Put the ramekins onto a baking sheet. Bake in the preheated oven for 15 minutes, or until risen, golden, and firm to the touch.

While the cupcakes are baking, make the meringue. Put the egg whites into a grease-free bowl and, using an electric mixer, beat until stiff. Gradually beat in the superfine sugar to form a stiff and glossy meringue.

Spread the lemon curd over the hot cupcakes, then swirl over the meringue. Return the cupcakes to the oven for 4–5 minutes, until the meringue is golden. Serve immediately.

Bouquet of Cupcakes

MAKES 16

generous 1 cup self-rising flour

¼ tsp baking powder

½ cup butter, softened, or soft margarine

generous ½ cup superfine sugar

2 eggs, lightly beaten

½ vanilla bean

2 tbsp milk

BUTTERCREAM

¾ cup unsalted butter, softened

1 tsp vanilla extract

2¾ cups confectioners' sugar

pink and purple food colorings

TO ASSEMBLE

4½-inch/12-cm floral foam (oasis) cube

white and pink tissue paper

6-inch/15-cm flowerpot toothpicks

fresh bay leaves

ribbon

Preheat the oven to 350°F/180°C. Put 16 paper liners into shallow muffin pans.

Sift the flour and baking powder into a large bowl. Add the butter, superfine sugar, eggs, seeds from the vanilla bean, and milk and, using an electric mixer, beat together until smooth.

Spoon the batter into the paper liners. Bake in the preheated oven for 15–20 minutes, until risen, golden, and firm to the touch. Transfer to a wire rack and let cool.

To make the buttercream, place the butter and vanilla extract in a bowl and beat with an electric mixer for 2–3 minutes, until pale and creamy. Gradually sift in the confectioners' sugar and continue beating for 2–3 minutes, until light and fluffy. Divide between two bowls and beat a little pink food coloring into one of the bowls and a little purple food coloring into the other.

Spoon each buttercream into a large pastry bag fitted with a medium star tip. Pipe swirls of pink buttercream over 8 of the cupcakes and purple buttercream over the remaining cupcakes. Chill for 30 minutes.

To assemble, use a sharp knife to trim off the corners of the floral foam cube. Wrap in a layer of white tissue paper and press into the flowerpot. Push two toothpicks into the bottom of each cupcake and gently push the cupcakes into the floral foam. Place a few bay leaves in between the cupcakes. Wrap the flowerpot in pink tissue paper and tie with ribbon.

Frosted Berry Cupcakes

MAKES 12

½ cup butter, softened, or soft margarine

generous ½ cup superfine sugar

2 tsp orange flower water

2 extra large eggs, lightly beaten

generous ½ cup ground almonds

scant 1 cup self-rising flour

2 tbsp milk

FROSTING

10½ oz/300 g mascarpone cheese

scant ½ cup superfine sugar

4 tbsp orange juice

TO DECORATE

2½ cups sugar-frosted mixed berries
(see page 42)

a few sugar-frosted fresh mint leaves (see page 42)

Preheat the oven to 350°F/180°C. Put 12 paper liners into a shallow muffin pan.

Place the butter, superfine sugar, and orange flower water in a large bowl and beat together until light and fluffy. Gradually beat in the eggs. Stir in the ground almonds. Sift in the flour and, using a metal spoon, fold in gently with the milk.

Spoon the batter into the paper liners. Bake in the preheated oven for 15–20 minutes, until risen, golden, and firm to the touch. Transfer to a wire rack and let cool.

To make the frosting, put the mascarpone cheese, superfine sugar, and orange juice in a bowl and beat together until smooth.

Swirl the frosting over the top of the cupcakes and arrange the sugar-frosted berries and mint leaves on top.

Gooey Chocolate & Cream Cheese Cupcakes

MAKES 12

generous 1⅓ cups all-purpose flour

scant ¼ cup unsweetened cocoa

¾ tsp baking soda

1 cup superfine sugar

4 tbsp sunflower oil

¾ cup water

2 tsp distilled white vinegar

½ tsp vanilla extract

⅔ cup cream cheese

1 egg, lightly beaten

½ cup semisweet chocolate chips

Preheat the oven to 350°F/180°C. Put 12 paper liners into a muffin pan.

Sift the flour, cocoa, and baking soda into a large bowl. Stir ¾ cup of the superfine sugar into the flour batter. Add the oil, water, vinegar, and vanilla extract and stir well until combined.

Place the remaining superfine sugar, the cream cheese, and egg in a large bowl and beat together until well mixed. Stir in the chocolate chips.

Spoon the cake batter into the paper liners and top each with a spoonful of the cream cheese batter. Bake in the preheated oven for 20–25 minutes, or until risen and firm to the touch. Transfer to a wire rack and let cool.

Caramel Cupcakes

MAKES 12

6 tbsp butter, softened, or soft margarine

¼ cup dark brown sugar

1 tbsp light corn syrup

1 extra large egg, lightly beaten

¾ cup self-rising flour

1 tsp freshly grated nutmeg

2 tbsp milk

TOPPING

generous ½ cup light brown sugar

1 medium egg white

1 tbsp hot water

pinch of cream of tartar

Preheat the oven to 350°F/180°C. Put 12 paper liners into a shallow muffin pan.

Place the butter, dark brown sugar, and corn syrup in a large bowl and beat together until light and fluffy. Gradually beat in the egg. Sift in the flour and nutmeg and, using a metal spoon, fold gently into the batter with the milk.

Spoon the batter into the paper liners. Bake in the preheated oven for 15–20 minutes, or until risen, golden, and firm to the touch. Transfer to a wire rack and let cool.

To make the topping, put all the ingredients in a heatproof bowl set over a saucepan of simmering water. Using an electric mixer, beat for 5–6 minutes, until the batter is thick and softly peaking when the beaters are lifted. Swirl the topping over the cupcakes.

Red Velvet Cupcakes

MAKES 12

generous 1 cup
all-purpose flour

1 tsp baking soda

2 tbsp unsweetened cocoa

½ cup butter, softened,
or soft margarine

scant ¾ cup superfine
sugar

1 extra large egg, lightly
beaten

½ cup buttermilk

1 tsp vanilla extract

1 tbsp red food coloring
liquid

FROSTING

⅔ cup cream cheese

6 tbsp unsalted butter,
softened

2¼ cups confectioners'
sugar

TO DECORATE

¼ cup granulated sugar

red food coloring paste

Preheat the oven to 350°F/180°C. Put 12 paper liners into a shallow muffin pan.

Sift together the flour, baking soda, and cocoa. Place the butter and superfine sugar in a separate large bowl and beat together until light and fluffy. Gradually beat in the egg and half of the flour batter. Beat in the buttermilk, vanilla extract, and red food coloring liquid. Fold in the remaining flour batter.

Spoon the batter into the paper liners. Bake the cupcakes in the preheated oven for 15–20 minutes, or until risen and firm to the touch. Transfer to a wire rack and let cool.

To make the frosting, put the cream cheese and butter in a bowl and blend together with a spatula. Sift in the confectioners' sugar and beat until smooth and creamy.

Place the granulated sugar and a little red food coloring paste in a plastic bag. Rub the bag between your fingers and thumb until well mixed. Swirl the frosting on the top of the cupcakes and sprinkle with the colored sugar.

Fudge & Raisin Cupcakes

MAKES 10

4 oz/115 g store-bought vanilla fudge, cut into small chunks

1 tbsp milk

6 tbsp butter, softened, or soft margarine

scant ¼ cup light brown sugar

1 extra large egg, lightly beaten

¾ cup self-rising flour

3 tbsp raisins

Preheat the oven to 375°F/190°C. Put 10 paper liners into a shallow muffin pan.

Put half of the fudge in a heatproof bowl with the milk, set over a saucepan of gently simmering water, and heat until the fudge has melted. Remove from the heat and stir until smooth. Let cool for 10 minutes.

Place the butter and brown sugar in a large bowl and beat together until light and fluffy. Gradually beat in the egg. Sift in the flour and, using a metal spoon, gently fold into the batter with the raisins. Fold in the melted fudge.

Spoon the batter into the paper liners. Scatter the remaining fudge chunks over the cupcakes. Bake in the preheated oven for 15–20 minutes, or until risen, golden, and firm to the touch. Transfer to a wire rack and let cool.

Gingerbread Cupcakes

MAKES 30

generous 1⅓ cups all-purpose flour

1 tbsp baking powder

2 tsp ground ginger

1 tsp ground cinnamon

¾ cup butter, softened, or soft margarine

scant 1 cup dark brown sugar

3 eggs, lightly beaten

1 tsp vanilla extract

chopped candied ginger, to decorate

BUTTERCREAM

6 tbsp unsalted butter, softened

3 tbsp orange juice

1¼ cups confectioners' sugar

Preheat the oven to 375°F/190°C. Put 30 paper liners into shallow muffin pans.

Sift the flour, baking powder, ground ginger, and cinnamon into a large bowl. Add the butter, brown sugar, eggs, and vanilla extract and, using an electric mixer, beat together until smooth.

Spoon the batter into the paper liners. Bake in the preheated oven for 15–20 minutes, or until risen, golden, and firm to the touch. Transfer to a wire rack and let cool.

To make the buttercream, place the butter and orange juice in a bowl and beat with an electric mixer until smooth. Sift in the confectioners' sugar and continue beating until light and fluffy. Spoon a little of the buttercream on top of each cupcake and scatter over the candied ginger.

Cherry Sundae Cupcakes

MAKES 12

¾ cup butter, softened, or soft margarine

scant 1 cup superfine sugar

3 eggs, lightly beaten

1 tsp vanilla extract

scant ⅔ cup all-purpose flour

1½ tsp baking powder

¼ cup chopped candied cherries

CHOCOLATE SAUCE

3 oz/85 g semisweet chocolate, broken into pieces

2 tbsp butter

1 tbsp light corn syrup

TO DECORATE

2½ cups heavy cream

2 tbsp toasted chopped mixed nuts

pink sanding sugar

12 maraschino cherries

Preheat the oven to 325°F/160°C. Put 12 paper liners into a muffin pan.

Place the butter and superfine sugar in a large bowl and beat together until light and fluffy. Gradually beat in the eggs and vanilla extract. Sift in the flour and baking powder and, using a metal spoon, fold in gently. Fold in the candied cherries.

Spoon the batter into the paper liners. Bake in the preheated oven for 25–30 minutes, until risen, golden, and firm to the touch. Transfer to a wire rack and let cool.

To make the chocolate sauce, place the chocolate, butter, and corn syrup in a heatproof bowl set over a saucepan of simmering water and heat until melted. Remove from the heat and stir until smooth. Let cool, stirring occasionally, for 20–30 minutes.

Whip the cream until holding firm peaks. Spoon into a pastry bag fitted with a large star tip and pipe large swirls of cream on top of each cupcake. Drizzle over the chocolate sauce and sprinkle with the chopped nuts and pink sugar. Top each with a maraschino cherry.

Butterscotch Cupcakes

MAKES 28

generous 1⅓ cups all-purpose flour

1 tbsp baking powder

¾ cup butter, softened, or soft margarine

scant 1 cup light brown sugar

3 eggs, lightly beaten

1 tsp vanilla extract

TOPPING

2 tbsp light corn syrup

2 tbsp unsalted butter

2 tbsp light brown sugar

Preheat the oven to 375°F/190°C. Put 28 paper liners into shallow muffin pans.

Sift the flour and baking powder into a large bowl. Add the butter, brown sugar, eggs, and vanilla extract and, using an electric mixer, beat together until smooth.

Spoon the batter into the paper liners. Bake in the preheated oven for 15–20 minutes, or until risen, golden, and firm to the touch. Transfer to a wire rack and let cool.

To make the topping, place the corn syrup, butter, and brown sugar in a small saucepan and heat gently, stirring, until the sugar dissolves. Bring to a boil and cook, stirring, for about 1 minute. Drizzle over the cupcakes and let set.

Coffee Fudge Cupcakes

MAKES 28

generous 1⅓ cups all-purpose flour

1 tbsp baking powder

¾ cup butter, softened, or soft margarine

scant 1 cup superfine sugar

3 eggs, lightly beaten

1 tsp coffee extract

2 tbsp milk

28 chocolate-covered coffee beans, to decorate

FROSTING

4 tbsp unsalted butter, softened

generous ½ cup light brown sugar

2 tbsp light cream or milk

½ tsp coffee extract

3¼ cups confectioners' sugar

Preheat the oven to 375°F/190°C. Put 28 paper liners into shallow muffin pans.

Sift the flour and baking powder into a large bowl. Add the butter, superfine sugar, eggs, and coffee extract and, using an electric mixer, beat together until smooth. Beat in the milk.

Spoon the batter into the paper liners. Bake in the preheated oven for 15–20 minutes, or until risen, golden, and firm to the touch. Transfer to a wire rack and let cool.

To make the frosting, place the butter, brown sugar, cream, and coffee extract in a saucepan over medium heat and stir until melted and smooth. Bring to a boil and cook, stirring, for 2 minutes. Remove from the heat and sift in the confectioners' sugar. Stir the frosting until smooth and thick.

Spoon the frosting into a pastry bag fitted with a large star tip. Pipe a swirl of frosting on top of each cupcake and top with a chocolate-covered coffee bean.

Pink Lemonade Cupcakes

MAKES 10

scant 1 cup self-rising flour

¼ tsp baking powder

½ cup butter, softened, or soft margarine

generous ½ cup superfine sugar

2 extra large eggs, lightly beaten

pink food coloring

¼ cup granulated sugar

juice of 1 small lemon

BUTTERCREAM

½ cup unsalted butter, softened

juice and finely grated rind of ½ lemon

4 tbsp heavy cream

1¾ cups confectioners' sugar

pink food coloring

TO DECORATE

pink, white, and red sugar sprinkles

10 pink or yellow drinking straws

Preheat the oven to 350°F/180°C. Put 10 paper liners into a shallow muffin pan.

Sift the flour and baking powder into a large bowl. Add the butter, superfine sugar, and eggs and, using an electric mixer, beat together until smooth. Beat in a little pink food coloring to color the batter pale pink.

Spoon the batter into the paper liners. Bake in the preheated oven for 15–20 minutes, until risen and firm to the touch.

Meanwhile, place the granulated sugar and lemon juice in a small saucepan and heat gently, stirring, until the sugar has dissolved. Let cool for 15 minutes. Prick the tops of the warm cupcakes all over with a skewer and liberally brush with the lemon syrup. Transfer to a wire rack and let cool.

To make the buttercream, place the butter, lemon juice, and lemon rind in a bowl and beat with an electric mixer for 2–3 minutes, until pale and creamy. Beat in the cream, then gradually sift in the confectioners' sugar and continue beating for 2–3 minutes, until the buttercream is light and fluffy. Beat in a little pink food coloring to give a pale pink color.

Using a small palette knife, thickly swirl the buttercream over the tops of the cupcakes. Scatter sugar sprinkles in the center of 5 of cupcakes and edge the remaining cupcakes with the sprinkles. Cut the straws to 3¼-inch/8-cm lengths and push into the cupcakes.

Peaches & Cream Cupcakes

MAKES 12

14 oz/400 g canned peach slices in fruit juice

½ cup butter, softened, or soft margarine

generous ½ cup superfine sugar

2 eggs, lightly beaten

scant 1 cup self-rising flour

⅔ cup heavy cream

Preheat the oven to 350°F/180°C. Put 12 paper liners into a muffin pan.

Drain the peaches, reserving the juice. Reserve 12 small slices and finely chop the remaining slices.

Place the butter and superfine sugar in a large bowl and beat together until light and fluffy. Gradually beat in the eggs. Sift in the flour and, using a metal spoon, fold in gently. Fold in the chopped peaches and 1 tablespoon of the reserved juice.

Spoon the batter into the paper liners. Bake in the preheated oven for 25 minutes, or until risen, golden, and firm to the touch. Transfer to a wire rack and let cool.

Whip the cream until holding soft peaks. Using a small palette knife, spread the cream over the cupcakes. Top with the reserved peach slices.

Lemon Cheesecake Cupcakes

MAKES 12

4½ tbsp butter, softened, or soft margarine

1 cup crushed graham crackers

scant ½ cup superfine sugar

1¼ cups cream cheese

2 extra large eggs, lightly beaten

finely grated rind of 1 large lemon

2 tsp lemon juice

½ cup sour cream

¼ cup all-purpose flour

2 small lemons, thinly sliced, to decorate

Preheat the oven to 325°F/160°C. Put 12 paper liners into a muffin pan.

Place the butter in a saucepan and heat gently until melted. Remove from the heat, then add the crushed crackers and 1 tablespoon of the superfine sugar and mix well. Spoon the crumb batter into the paper liners and press down firmly with the back of a teaspoon. Chill in the refrigerator.

Meanwhile, place the remaining superfine sugar, the cream cheese, and eggs in a large bowl and beat together until smooth. Add the lemon rind, lemon juice, and sour cream and beat together until combined. Add the flour and beat well.

Spoon the cream cheese mixture into the paper liners. Bake in the preheated oven for 30 minutes, or until set but not browned. Transfer to a wire rack and let cool.

When the cupcakes are cold, chill in the refrigerator for at least 3 hours. Decorate each cupcake with a twisted lemon slice.

Neapolitan Cupcakes

MAKES 12

generous 1 cup self-rising flour

½ tsp baking powder

generous ½ cup butter, softened, or soft margarine

¾ cup superfine sugar

2 extra large eggs, lightly beaten

1 tsp vanilla extract

1 tbsp milk

1 tbsp unsweetened cocoa mixed to a paste with 1½ tbsp hot water

FROSTING

¾ cup cream cheese

½ cup unsalted butter, softened

2¾ cups confectioners' sugar

1 tbsp strawberry jelly

pink food coloring

TO DECORATE

chocolate sprinkles

6 ice-cream cone wafers, each cut into 4 triangles

Preheat the oven to 350°F/180°C. Put 12 paper liners into a muffin pan.

Sift the flour and baking powder into a large bowl. Add the butter, superfine sugar, and eggs and, using an electric mixer, beat together until smooth.

Divide the batter between two bowls. Beat the vanilla extract and milk into one of the bowls and the cocoa paste into the other bowl.

Place alternate teaspoonfuls of the batters into the paper liners. Bake in the preheated oven for 15–20 minutes, until risen and firm to the touch. Transfer to a wire rack and let cool.

To make the frosting, put the cream cheese and butter in a bowl and blend together with a spatula. Sift in the confectioners' sugar and beat until smooth and creamy. Divide the frosting between two bowls and stir the jelly and a little pink food coloring into one of the bowls. Cover and chill both bowls of frosting in the refrigerator for 30 minutes.

Place alternate spoonfuls of the frostings into a large pastry bag fitted with a large star tip. Pipe swirls of the frosting on the top of each cupcake. Sprinkle with chocolate sprinkles and decorate each cupcake with 2 wafer triangles.

Sticky Date Cupcakes

MAKES 6

½ cup chopped pitted dried dates

½ tsp baking soda

scant ½ cup water

6 tbsp butter, softened, or soft margarine, plus extra for greasing

scant ½ cup dark brown sugar

1 tsp vanilla extract

2 eggs, lightly beaten

scant 1 cup self-rising flour

whipped heavy cream, to serve

CARAMEL SAUCE

scant ½ cup dark brown sugar

4 tbsp butter

4 tbsp heavy cream

Preheat the oven to 350°F/180°C. Grease six ⅔-cup ramekins or individual baking dishes.

Put the dates, baking soda, and water in a small saucepan and bring to a boil. Remove from the heat and set aside to cool.

Place the butter, brown sugar, and vanilla extract in a large bowl and beat together until light and fluffy. Gradually beat in the eggs. Sift in the flour and, using a metal spoon, fold into the batter, followed by the date mixture.

Spoon the batter into the ramekins. Put the ramekins on a baking sheet. Bake in the preheated oven for 20–25 minutes, or until risen and firm to the touch.

To make the caramel sauce, put all the ingredients in a small saucepan and heat until the butter has melted. Simmer for 5 minutes, stirring occasionally. Using a skewer, prick a few holes in each warm cupcake and drizzle over some of the sauce. Top with a little whipped cream and serve with the remaining caramel sauce.

Warm Molten-Centered Chocolate Cupcakes

MAKES 8

2/3 cup self-rising flour

1 tbsp unsweetened cocoa

4 tbsp butter, softened, or soft margarine

1/4 cup superfine sugar

1 extra large egg, lightly beaten

2 oz/55 g semisweet chocolate

confectioners' sugar, for dusting

Preheat the oven to 375°F/190°C. Put 8 paper liners into a shallow muffin pan.

Sift the flour and cocoa into a large bowl. Add the butter, superfine sugar, and egg and, using an electric mixer, beat together until smooth.

Spoon half of the batter into the paper liners. Using a teaspoon, make an indentation in the center of each. Break the chocolate into 8 equal-size squares and place a piece in each indentation, then spoon the remaining cake batter on top.

Bake in the preheated oven for 20 minutes, or until risen and firm to the touch. Let the cupcakes cool in the pan for 2–3 minutes before serving warm, dusted with confectioners' sugar.

Tiramisu Cupcakes

MAKES 12

scant 1 cup self-rising flour

½ tsp baking powder

½ cup butter, softened, or soft margarine

½ cup light brown sugar

2 eggs, lightly beaten

2 tbsp finely grated semisweet chocolate, to decorate

COFFEE SYRUP

2 tsp instant coffee powder

2 tbsp confectioners' sugar

4 tbsp water

FROSTING

8 oz/225 g mascarpone cheese

scant ½ cup superfine sugar

2 tbsp Marsala wine or sweet sherry

Preheat the oven to 350°F/180°C. Put 12 paper liners into a shallow muffin pan.

Sift the flour and baking powder into a large bowl. Add the butter, brown sugar, and eggs and, using an electric mixer, beat together until smooth.

Spoon the batter into the paper liners. Bake in the preheated oven for 15–20 minutes, or until risen, golden, and firm to the touch.

Meanwhile, make the coffee syrup. Put the coffee powder, confectioners' sugar, and water in a saucepan and heat gently, stirring, until the coffee and sugar have dissolved. Boil for 1 minute, then let cool for 10 minutes.

Prick the tops of the warm cupcakes over all over with a skewer and brush with the coffee syrup. Transfer to a wire rack and let cool.

To make the frosting, put the mascarpone cheese, superfine sugar, and Marsala wine in a bowl and beat together until smooth. Spread over the top of the cupcakes. Using a star stencil, sprinkle the grated chocolate over the frosting.

Ultimate Chocolate Cupcakes

MAKES 14

scant 1 cup self-rising flour

½ tsp baking powder

1½ tbsp unsweetened cocoa

½ cup butter, softened, or soft margarine

generous ½ cup superfine sugar

2 extra large eggs, lightly beaten

2 oz/55 g semisweet chocolate, melted

FROSTING

5½ oz/150 g semisweet chocolate, finely chopped

scant 1 cup heavy cream

scant ¾ cup unsalted butter, softened

2¼ cups confectioners' sugar

TO DECORATE

piped chocolate shapes (see page 37)

gold dragées

Preheat the oven to 350°F/180°C. Put 14 paper liners into shallow muffin pans.

Sift the flour, baking powder, and cocoa into a large bowl. Add the butter, superfine sugar, and eggs and, using an electric mixer, beat together until smooth. Fold in the melted chocolate.

Spoon the batter into the paper liners. Bake in the preheated oven for 15–20 minutes, or until risen and firm to the touch. Transfer to a wire rack and let cool.

To make the frosting, put the chocolate in a heatproof bowl. Heat the cream in a saucepan until boiling, then pour over the chocolate and stir until smooth. Let cool for 20 minutes, stirring occasionally, until thickened. Put the butter in a bowl, sift in the confectioners' sugar, and beat until smooth. Beat in the chocolate mixture. Chill for 15–20 minutes.

Spoon the frosting into a pastry bag fitted with a large star tip. Pipe swirls of frosting on top of each cupcake. Decorate with piped chocolate shapes and gold dragées.

Chocolate Brownie Cupcakes

MAKES 12

8 oz/225 g semisweet chocolate, broken into pieces

6 tbsp butter, softened, or soft margarine

2 extra large eggs, lightly beaten

1 cup dark brown sugar

1 tsp vanilla extract

generous 1 cup all-purpose flour

²/₃ cup chopped walnuts

Preheat the oven to 350°F/180°C. Put 12 paper liners into a muffin pan.

Place the chocolate and butter in a saucepan and heat gently, stirring continuously, until melted. Remove from the heat and stir until smooth. Let cool slightly.

Place the eggs and brown sugar in a large bowl and beat together, then add the vanilla extract. Sift in the flour and fold in gently, then stir in the melted chocolate mixture until combined. Stir in the chopped walnuts.

Spoon the batter into the paper liners. Bake in the preheated oven for 30 minutes, or until firm to the touch but still slightly moist in the center. Transfer to a wire rack and let cool.

Double Chocolate Cupcakes

MAKES 18

3 oz/85 g white chocolate, broken into pieces

1 tbsp milk

scant 1 cup self-rising flour

½ tsp baking powder

½ cup butter, softened, or soft margarine

generous ½ cup superfine sugar

2 eggs, lightly beaten

1 tsp vanilla extract

TOPPING

5 oz/140 g milk chocolate, broken into pieces

18 white chocolate disks

Preheat the oven to 375°F/190°C. Put 18 paper liners into shallow muffin pans.

Place the white chocolate in a heatproof bowl and add the milk. Set the bowl over a saucepan of simmering water and heat until melted. Remove from the heat and stir gently until smooth.

Sift the flour and baking powder into a large bowl. Add the butter, superfine sugar, eggs, and vanilla extract and, using an electric mixer, beat together until smooth. Fold in the melted white chocolate mixture.

Spoon the batter into the paper liners. Bake in the preheated oven for 20 minutes, or until risen, golden, and firm to the touch. Transfer to a wire rack and let cool.

To make the topping, place the chocolate in a heatproof bowl and set the bowl over a saucepan of gently simmering water until melted. Let cool for 5 minutes, then spread over the tops of the cupcakes. Decorate each cupcake with a chocolate disk.

Mocha Cupcakes

MAKES 20

2 tbsp instant espresso coffee powder

6 tbsp butter, softened, or soft margarine

scant ½ cup superfine sugar

1 tbsp honey

scant 1 cup water

1¾ cups all-purpose flour

2 tbsp unsweetened cocoa

1 tsp baking soda

3 tbsp milk

1 extra large egg, lightly beaten

TOPPING

1 cup heavy cream

unsweetened cocoa, for dusting

Preheat the oven to 350°F/180°C. Put 20 paper liners into shallow muffin pans.

Put the coffee powder, butter, superfine sugar, honey, and water in a saucepan and heat gently, stirring, until the sugar has dissolved. Bring to a boil, then reduce the heat and simmer for 5 minutes. Pour into a large heatproof bowl and let cool.

When the mixture has cooled, sift in the flour and cocoa. Dissolve the baking soda in the milk, then add to the mixture with the egg and beat together until smooth.

Spoon the batter into the paper liners. Bake in the preheated oven for 15–20 minutes, or until risen and firm to the touch. Transfer to a wire rack and let cool.

To make the topping, whip the cream in a bowl until it hold its shape. Spoon a teaspoonful of cream on top of each cupcake, then dust with cocoa.

Chocolate & Hazelnut Cupcakes

MAKES 18

¾ cup butter, softened, or soft margarine

generous ½ cup light brown sugar

2 extra large eggs, lightly beaten

2 tbsp chocolate hazelnut spread

1⅓ cups self-rising flour

generous ½ cup roughly ground, blanched hazelnuts

TOPPING

5 tbsp chocolate hazelnut spread

18 whole blanched hazelnuts

Preheat the oven to 350°F/180°C. Put 18 paper liners into shallow muffin pans.

Put the butter and brown sugar in a large bowl and beat together until light and fluffy. Gradually beat in the eggs, then stir in the chocolate hazelnut spread. Sift in the flour and, using a metal spoon, fold into the batter with the ground hazelnuts.

Spoon the batter into the paper liners. Bake in the preheated oven for 20–25 minutes, or until risen and firm to the touch. Transfer to a wire rack and let cool.

Spread the chocolate hazelnut spread over the cupcakes and top each with a blanched hazelnut.

Chocolate & Orange Cupcakes

MAKES 16

½ cup butter, softened, or soft margarine

generous ½ cup superfine sugar

finely grated rind and juice of ½ orange

2 eggs, lightly beaten

scant 1 cup self-rising flour

¼ cup grated semisweet chocolate

thin strips of candied orange peel, to decorate

FROSTING

4 oz/115 g semisweet chocolate, broken into pieces

2 tbsp unsalted butter

1 tbsp light corn syrup

Preheat the oven to 350°F/180°C. Put 16 paper liners into shallow muffin pans.

Put the butter, superfine sugar, and orange rind in a large bowl and beat together until light and fluffy. Gradually beat in the eggs. Sift in the flour and, using a metal spoon, fold gently into the batter with the orange juice and grated chocolate.

Spoon the batter into the paper liners. Bake in the preheated oven for 20 minutes, or until risen, golden, and firm to the touch. Transfer to a wire rack and let cool.

To make the frosting, place the chocolate in a heatproof bowl and add the butter and corn syrup. Set the bowl over a saucepan of simmering water and heat until melted. Remove from the heat and stir until smooth. Let cool until the frosting is thick enough to spread.

Spread the frosting over the cupcakes and decorate each with a few strips of candied orange peel. Let set.

Chocolate Cupcakes with Cream Cheese Frosting

MAKES 18

6 tbsp butter, softened, or soft margarine

½ cup superfine sugar

2 eggs, lightly beaten

1¾ cups self-rising flour

¼ cup unsweetened cocoa

2 tbsp milk

⅓ cup semisweet chocolate chips

chocolate curls, to decorate

FROSTING

8 oz/225 g white chocolate, broken into pieces

⅔ cup low-fat cream cheese

Preheat the oven to 400°F/200°C. Put 18 paper liners into shallow muffin pans.

Place the butter and superfine sugar in a large bowl and beat together until light and fluffy. Gradually beat in the eggs. Sift in the flour and cocoa and, using a metal spoon, fold gently into the batter with the milk and chocolate chips.

Spoon the batter into the paper liners. Bake in the preheated oven for 20 minutes, or until risen and firm to the touch. Transfer to a wire rack and let cool.

To make the frosting, place the chocolate in a heatproof bowl and set the bowl over a saucepan of simmering water until melted. Let cool slightly. Put the cream cheese in a bowl and beat until softened, then beat in the melted chocolate.

Spread a little of the frosting over the top of each cupcake and decorate with chocolate curls. Let chill in the refrigerator for 1 hour before serving.

Pear & Chocolate Cupcakes

MAKES 12

¾ cup self-rising flour

½ tsp baking powder

2 tbsp unsweetened cocoa

½ cup butter, softened, or soft margarine

generous ½ cup light brown sugar

2 eggs, lightly beaten

4 canned pear halves, drained and sliced

2 tbsp honey, warmed

Preheat the oven to 375°F/190°C. Put 12 paper liners into a shallow muffin pan.

Sift the flour, baking powder, and cocoa into a large bowl. Add the butter, brown sugar, and eggs and, using an electric mixer, beat together until smooth.

Spoon the batter into the paper liners. Arrange the pear slices on top of the cupcakes. Bake in the preheated oven for 20 minutes, or until risen and firm to the touch. Transfer to a wire rack and, while still warm, glaze with the honey. Let cool.

Chocolate-Topped Cupcakes

MAKES 30

1⅓ cups all-purpose flour

1 tbsp baking powder

¾ cup butter, softened, or soft margarine

scant 1 cup superfine sugar

3 eggs, lightly beaten

1 tsp vanilla extract

2 tbsp milk

1 tbsp unsweetened cocoa

½ cup grated milk chocolate

3 tbsp apricot jelly, warmed

Preheat the oven to 375°F/190°C. Put 30 paper liners into shallow muffin pans.

Sift the flour and baking powder into a large bowl. Add the butter, superfine sugar, eggs, and vanilla extract and, using an electric mixer, beat together until smooth. Mix the milk with the cocoa and stir into the batter.

Spoon the batter into the paper liners and sprinkle with about one quarter of the grated chocolate. Bake in the preheated oven for 15–20 minutes, or until risen and firm to the touch. Transfer to a wire rack and let cool.

When the cupcakes are cold, brush the tops with the jelly and sprinkle with the remaining grated chocolate.

Chocolate Paradise Cupcakes

MAKES 16

3 oz/85 g semisweet chocolate, broken into pieces

4 tbsp milk

1 tbsp unsweetened cocoa

½ cup butter, softened, or soft margarine

generous ½ cup dark brown sugar

2 extra large eggs, lightly beaten

3 tbsp sour cream

1⅓ cups all-purpose flour

½ tsp baking soda

TOPPING

16 white marshmallows

3 tbsp milk

1¼ cups heavy cream

generous ½ cup unsweetened dried shredded coconut

2 oz/55 g semisweet chocolate, melted

Preheat the oven to 350°F/180°C. Put 16 paper liners into shallow muffin pans.

Place the chocolate, milk, and cocoa in a heatproof bowl set over a saucepan of simmering water and heat until the chocolate has melted. Remove from the heat and stir until smooth.

Place the butter and brown sugar in a large bowl and beat together until light and fluffy. Gradually beat in the eggs, then beat in the melted chocolate mixture and sour cream. Sift in the flour and baking soda and, using a metal spoon, fold in gently.

Spoon the batter into the paper liners. Bake in the preheated oven for 18–20 minutes, or until risen and firm to the touch. Transfer to a wire rack and let cool.

To make the topping, place the marshmallows and milk in a heatproof bowl set over a saucepan of simmering water. Let heat until the marshmallows have melted, stirring occasionally. Remove from the heat and let cool. Whip the cream until holding firm peaks, then fold into the marshmallow mixture with ⅓ cup of the coconut. Cover and chill in the refrigerator for 30 minutes.

Spread the topping on top of the cupcakes. Sprinkle over the remaining coconut. Spoon the melted chocolate into a small paper pastry bag, snip off the end, and pipe crisscross lines over the top of each cupcake. Let set.

Chocolate Toffee Cupcakes

MAKES 30

1⅓ cups all-purpose flour

1 tbsp baking powder

¾ cup butter, softened, or soft margarine

scant 1 cup superfine sugar

3 eggs, lightly beaten

1 tsp vanilla extract

3 oz/85 g chocolate-covered sponge toffee, finely chopped

ICING

1⅔ cups confectioners' sugar

2 tsp unsweetened cocoa

about 2 tbsp water

Preheat the oven to 375°F/190°C. Put 30 paper liners into shallow muffin pans.

Sift the flour and baking powder into a large bowl. Add the butter, superfine sugar, eggs, and vanilla extract and, using an electric mixer, beat together until smooth. Stir in half of the sponge toffee.

Spoon the batter into the paper liners. Bake in the preheated oven for 15–20 minutes, or until risen, golden, and firm to the touch. Transfer to a wire rack and let cool.

To make the icing, sift the confectioners' sugar and cocoa into a bowl and stir in the water to make a smooth paste. Spoon the icing over the cupcakes and top with the remaining sponge toffee. Let set.

Dark & Light Cupcakes

MAKES 20

scant 1 cup water

6 tbsp butter

scant ½ cup superfine sugar

1 tbsp light corn syrup

3 tbsp milk

1 tsp vanilla extract

1 tsp baking soda

1¾ cups all-purpose flour

2 tbsp unsweetened cocoa

semisweet and white chocolate shavings, to decorate

FROSTING

1¾ oz/50 g semisweet chocolate, broken into pieces

4 tbsp water

3½ tbsp unsalted butter

1¾ oz/50 g white chocolate, broken into pieces

2¾ cups confectioners' sugar

Preheat the oven to 350°F/180°C. Put 20 paper liners into shallow muffin pans.

Place the water, butter, superfine sugar, and corn syrup in a saucepan and heat gently, stirring, until the sugar has dissolved. Bring to a boil, then reduce the heat and simmer gently for 5 minutes. Let cool.

Meanwhile, place the milk and vanilla extract in a small bowl. Add the baking soda and stir to dissolve. Sift the flour and cocoa into a separate large bowl and add the syrup mixture. Stir in the milk mixture and beat until smooth.

Spoon the batter into the paper liners. Bake in the preheated oven for 20 minutes, or until risen and firm to the touch. Transfer to a wire rack and let cool.

To make the frosting, place the semisweet chocolate in a small heatproof bowl with 2 tablespoons of the water and half of the butter. Set the bowl over a saucepan of gently simmering water and heat until melted. Stir until smooth and then let stand over the water. Repeat with the white chocolate and remaining water and butter. Sift half of the confectioners' sugar into each bowl and beat until smooth and thick.

Top half of the cupcakes with the semisweet chocolate frosting and half with the white chocolate frosting. Decorate with chocolate shavings and let set.

Chocolate Chip Cupcakes

MAKES 12

¾ cup self-rising flour

7 tbsp butter, softened, or soft margarine

½ cup superfine sugar

2 extra large eggs, lightly beaten

generous ½ cup semisweet chocolate chips

Preheat the oven to 375°F/190°C. Put 12 paper liners into a shallow muffin pan.

Sift the flour into a large bowl. Add the butter, superfine sugar, and eggs and, using an electric mixer, beat together until smooth. Fold in the chocolate chips.

Spoon the batter into the paper liners. Bake in the preheated oven for 20–25 minutes, or until risen, golden, and firm to the touch. Transfer to a wire rack and let cool.

Devil's Food Cupcakes

MAKES 18

scant 1 cup all-purpose flour

½ tsp baking soda

¼ cup unsweetened cocoa

3½ tbsp butter, softened, or soft margarine

generous ½ cup dark brown sugar

2 extra large eggs, lightly beaten

½ cup sour cream

chocolate caraque, to decorate

FROSTING

4½ oz/125 g semisweet chocolate, broken into pieces

2 tbsp superfine sugar

⅔ cup sour cream

Preheat the oven to 350°F/180°C. Put 18 paper liners into shallow muffin pans.

Sift the flour, baking soda, and cocoa into a large bowl. Add the butter, brown sugar, and eggs and, using an electric mixer, beat together until smooth. Fold in the sour cream.

Spoon the batter into the paper liners. Bake in the preheated oven for 20 minutes, or until risen and firm to the touch. Transfer to a wire rack and let cool.

To make the frosting, place the chocolate in a heatproof bowl. Set the bowl over a saucepan of gently simmering water and heat until melted, stirring occasionally. Remove from the heat and let cool slightly, then beat in the superfine sugar and sour cream until combined.

Spread the frosting over the tops of the cupcakes and decorate with chocolate caraque. Let set.

Tiny Chocolate Cupcakes

MAKES 20

4 tbsp butter, softened, or soft margarine

¼ cup superfine sugar

1 extra large egg, lightly beaten

scant ½ cup self-rising flour

2 tbsp unsweetened cocoa

1 tbsp milk

20 chocolate-covered coffee beans, to decorate

FROSTING

3½ oz/100 g semisweet chocolate, broken into pieces

scant ½ cup heavy cream

Preheat the oven to 375°F/190°C. Put 20 miniature paper liners into a miniature muffin pan.

Place the butter and superfine sugar in a large bowl and beat together until light and fluffy. Gradually beat in the egg. Sift in the flour and cocoa and, using a metal spoon, fold in gently. Stir in the milk.

Spoon the batter into the paper liners. Bake in the preheated oven for 10–15 minutes, or until risen and firm to the touch. Transfer to a wire rack and let cool.

To make the frosting, place the chocolate in a saucepan and add the cream. Heat gently, stirring all the time, until the chocolate has melted. Pour into a large heatproof bowl and, using an electric mixer, beat the mixture for 10 minutes, or until thick, glossy, and cool.

Spoon the frosting into a pastry bag fitted with a large star tip. Pipe a swirl of frosting on top of each cupcake and decorate with a chocolate-covered coffee bean. Chill in the refrigerator for 1 hour before serving.

White Chocolate & Rose Cupcakes

MAKES 12

½ cup butter, softened, or soft margarine

generous ½ cup superfine sugar

1 tsp rose water

2 eggs, lightly beaten

scant 1 cup self-rising flour

scant ½ cup grated white chocolate

sugar-frosted rose petals, to decorate (see page 42)

FROSTING

4 oz/115 g white chocolate, broken into pieces

2 tbsp milk

¾ cup cream cheese

scant ¼ cup confectioners' sugar

Preheat the oven to 350°F/180°C. Put 12 paper liners into a shallow muffin pan.

Place the butter, superfine sugar, and rose water in a large bowl and beat together until light and fluffy. Gradually beat in the eggs. Sift in the flour and, using a metal spoon, fold in gently. Fold in the grated chocolate.

Spoon the batter into the paper liners. Bake in the preheated oven for 15–20 minutes, or until risen, golden, and firm to the touch. Transfer to a wire rack and let cool.

To make the frosting, place the chocolate and milk in a heatproof bowl set over a saucepan of simmering water and let heat until melted. Remove from the heat and stir until smooth. Let cool for 30 minutes. Put the cream cheese in a separate bowl, sift in the confectioners' sugar, and beat together until smooth and creamy. Fold in the melted chocolate. Chill in the refrigerator for 1 hour.

Swirl the frosting over the tops of the cupcakes. Decorate with sugar-frosted rose petals.

Fruit & Nut

Banana & Pecan Cupcakes

MAKES 24

½ cup butter, softened, or soft margarine

generous ½ cup superfine sugar

½ tsp vanilla extract

2 eggs, lightly beaten

2 ripe bananas, mashed

¼ cup sour cream

1¾ cups all-purpose flour

1¼ tsp baking powder

¼ tsp baking soda

½ cup roughly chopped pecans

24 pecan halves, to decorate

BUTTERCREAM

½ cup unsalted butter, softened

1⅓ cups confectioners' sugar

Preheat the oven to 375°F/190°C. Put 24 paper liners into shallow muffin pans.

Place the butter, superfine sugar, and vanilla extract in a large bowl and beat together until light and fluffy. Gradually beat in the eggs. Stir in the mashed bananas and sour cream. Sift in the flour, baking powder, and baking soda and, using a metal spoon, fold into the batter with the chopped pecans.

Spoon the batter into the paper liners. Bake in the preheated oven for 20 minutes, or until risen, golden, and firm to the touch. Transfer to a wire rack and let cool.

To make the buttercream, put the butter in a bowl and beat until fluffy. Sift in the confectioners' sugar and mix together well.

Spoon the buttercream into a large pastry bag fitted with a large star tip. Pipe a swirl of buttercream on top of each cupcake and decorate with a pecan half.

Raspberry Almond Cupcakes

MAKES 14

½ cup butter, softened, or soft margarine

scant ½ cup superfine sugar

½ tsp almond extract

2 eggs, lightly beaten

⅔ cup self-rising flour

generous ½ cup ground almonds

¾ cup fresh raspberries

2 tbsp slivered almonds

confectioners' sugar, for dusting

Preheat the oven to 350°/180°C. Put 14 paper liners into shallow muffin pans.

Place the butter, superfine sugar, and almond extract in a large bowl and beat together until light and fluffy. Gradually beat in the eggs. Sift in the flour and, using a metal spoon, fold into the batter with the ground almonds. Gently fold in the raspberries.

Spoon the batter into the paper liners. Scatter the slivered almonds over the top. Bake in the preheated oven for 25–30 minutes, or until risen, golden, and firm to the touch. Transfer to a wire rack and let cool. Dust with confectioners' sugar.

Blueberry Cupcakes with Sour Cream Icing

MAKES 30

1⅓ cups all-purpose flour

1 tbsp baking powder

¾ cup butter, softened, or soft margarine

scant 1 cup superfine sugar

3 eggs, lightly beaten

1 tsp vanilla extract

finely grated rind of ½ orange

1 cup fresh blueberries

ICING

1¼ cups confectioners' sugar

3 tbsp sour cream

Preheat the oven to 375°F/190°C. Put 30 paper liners into shallow muffin pans.

Sift the flour and baking powder into a large bowl. Add the butter, superfine sugar, eggs, and vanilla extract and, using an electric mixer, beat together until smooth. Stir in the orange rind and scant ¾ cup of the blueberries.

Spoon the batter into the paper liners. Bake in the preheated oven for 15–20 minutes, or until risen, golden, and firm to the touch. Transfer to a wire rack and let cool.

To make the icing, sift the confectioners' sugar into a bowl and stir in the sour cream. Spoon a little of the icing on top of each cupcake and decorate with the remaining blueberries. Let set.

Frosted Peanut Butter Cupcakes

MAKES 16

4 tbsp butter, softened, or soft margarine

generous 1 cup light brown sugar

½ cup chunky peanut butter

2 eggs, lightly beaten

1 tsp vanilla extract

1¾ cups all-purpose flour

2 tsp baking powder

scant ½ cup milk

chopped unsalted peanuts, to decorate

FROSTING

scant 1 cup cream cheese

2 tbsp unsalted butter, softened

1¾ cups confectioners' sugar

Preheat the oven to 350°/180°C. Put 16 paper liners into shallow muffin pans.

Place the butter, brown sugar, and peanut butter in a large bowl and beat together for 1–2 minutes, or until well mixed. Gradually beat in the eggs, then add the vanilla extract. Sift in the flour and baking powder and, using a metal spoon, fold into the batter with the milk.

Spoon the batter into the paper liners. Bake in the preheated oven for 25 minutes, or until risen, golden, and firm to the touch. Transfer to a wire rack and let cool.

To make the frosting, put the cream cheese and butter in a bowl and beat together until smooth. Sift the confectioners' sugar into the mixture and mix well.

Spoon the frosting into a pastry bag fitted with a large star tip. Pipe a swirl of frosting on top of each cupcake and decorate with the chopped peanuts.

Vanilla, Hazelnut & Yogurt Cupcakes

MAKES 26

1⅓ cups all-purpose flour

2 tsp cornstarch

1 tbsp baking powder

¾ cup plain yogurt

scant 1 cup superfine sugar

3 eggs, lightly beaten

1 tsp vanilla extract

⅓ cup finely chopped hazelnuts

roughly chopped hazelnuts, to decorate

ICING

generous ¾ cup confectioners' sugar

3 tbsp plain yogurt

Preheat the oven to 375°F/190°C. Put 26 paper liners into shallow muffin pans.

Sift the flour, cornstarch, and baking powder into a large bowl. Add the yogurt, superfine sugar, eggs, and vanilla extract and, using an electric mixer, beat together until smooth. Stir in the finely chopped hazelnuts.

Spoon the batter into the paper liners. Bake in the preheated oven for 15–20 minutes, or until risen, golden, and firm to the touch. Transfer to a wire rack and let cool.

To make the icing, sift the confectioners' sugar into a bowl and stir in the yogurt. Drizzle over the cupcakes and sprinkle with roughly chopped hazelnuts. Let set.

Mango & Passion Fruit Cupcakes

MAKES 18

½ cup butter, softened, or soft margarine

generous ½ cup superfine sugar

1 tsp finely grated orange rind

2 eggs, lightly beaten

scant 1 cup self-rising flour

⅓ cup finely chopped dried mango

1 tbsp orange juice

ICING

1⅔ cups confectioners' sugar

seeds and pulp from 1 passion fruit

1–2 tbsp orange juice

Preheat the oven to 375°F/190°C. Put 18 paper liners into shallow muffin pans.

Place the butter, superfine sugar, and orange rind in a large bowl and beat together until light and fluffy. Gradually beat in the eggs. Sift in the flour and, using a metal spoon, fold into the batter with the mango and orange juice.

Spoon the batter into the paper liners. Bake in the preheated oven for 20 minutes, or until risen, golden, and firm to the touch. Transfer to a wire rack and let cool.

To make the icing, sift the confectioners' sugar into a bowl and add the passion fruit seeds and pulp and 1 tablespoon of the orange juice. Mix to a smooth icing, adding more orange juice, if necessary. Spoon the icing over the cupcakes. Let set.

Hummingbird Cupcakes

MAKES 12

1¼ cups all-purpose flour

¾ tsp baking soda

1 tsp ground cinnamon

⅔ cup light brown sugar

2 eggs, lightly beaten

scant ½ cup sunflower oil

1 ripe banana, mashed

2 canned pineapple rings, drained and finely chopped

¼ cup finely chopped pecans

12 pecan pieces, to decorate

FROSTING

⅔ cup cream cheese

5 tbsp unsalted butter, softened

1 tsp vanilla extract

2¼ cups confectioners' sugar

Preheat the oven to 350°/180°C. Put 12 paper liners into a shallow muffin pan.

Sift the flour, baking soda, and cinnamon into a bowl and stir in the brown sugar. Add the eggs, oil, banana, pineapple, and chopped pecans and mix thoroughly.

Spoon the batter into the paper liners. Bake in the preheated oven for 15–20 minutes, or until risen, golden, and firm to the touch. Transfer to a wire rack and let cool.

To make the frosting, put the cream cheese, butter, and vanilla extract in a bowl and blend together with a spatula. Sift in the confectioners' sugar and beat until smooth and creamy.

Spoon the frosting into a pastry bag fitted with a large star tip. Pipe a wavy line of frosting on top of each cupcake and decorate with pecan pieces.

Carrot Cake Cupcakes

MAKES 12

¾ cup butter, softened, or soft margarine

generous ½ cup superfine sugar

2 eggs, lightly beaten

2¾ cups grated carrot

scant ½ cup finely chopped walnuts,

2 tbsp orange juice

grated rind of ½ orange

1⅓ cups self-rising flour

1 tsp ground cinnamon

12 walnut halves, to decorate

FROSTING

½ cup cream cheese

1 tbsp orange juice

1¾ cups confectioners' sugar

Preheat the oven to 350°/180°C. Put 12 paper liners into a muffin pan.

Place the butter and superfine sugar in a large bowl and beat together until light and fluffy. Gradually beat in the eggs. Fold in the carrot, chopped walnuts, orange juice, and orange rind. Sift in the flour and cinnamon and, using a metal spoon, fold in gently.

Spoon the batter into the paper liners. Bake in the preheated oven for 15–20 minutes, or until risen, golden, and firm to the touch. Transfer to a wire rack and let cool.

To make the frosting, put the cream cheese and orange juice in a bowl. Sift in the confectioners' sugar and beat until fluffy. Spread the frosting over the cupcakes and top each with a walnut half.

Macadamia & Maple Cupcakes

MAKES 10

6 tbsp butter, softened, or soft margarine

¼ cup light brown sugar

2 tbsp maple syrup

1 extra large egg, lightly beaten

⅔ cup self-rising flour

⅓ cup chopped macadamia nuts

1 tbsp milk

2 tbsp lightly toasted chopped macadamia nuts, to decorate

FROSTING

2 tbsp unsalted butter, softened

2 tbsp maple syrup

⅔ cup confectioners' sugar

⅓ cup cream cheese

Preheat the oven to 375°F/190°C. Put 10 paper liners into a shallow muffin pan.

Place the butter, brown sugar, and maple syrup in a large bowl and beat together until light and fluffy. Gradually beat in the egg. Sift in the flour and, using a metal spoon, fold into the batter with the nuts and milk.

Spoon the batter into the paper liners. Bake in the preheated oven for 20 minutes, or until risen, golden, and firm to the touch. Transfer to a wire rack and let cool.

To make the frosting, beat the butter and maple syrup together until smooth. Sift in the confectioners' sugar and beat in thoroughly. Gently beat in the cream cheese. Swirl the frosting on top of the cupcakes and decorate with the toasted nuts.

Apple Streusel Cupcakes

MAKES 14

½ tsp baking soda

1¼ cups applesauce

4 tbsp butter, softened, or soft margarine

scant ½ cup raw brown sugar

1 extra large egg, lightly beaten

1⅓ cups self-rising flour

½ tsp ground cinnamon

½ tsp freshly grated nutmeg

TOPPING

⅓ cup all-purpose flour

¼ cup raw brown sugar

¼ tsp ground cinnamon

¼ tsp freshly grated nutmeg

2½ tbsp butter

Preheat the oven to 350°/180°C. Put 14 paper liners into shallow muffin pans.

To make the topping, put the flour, raw brown sugar, cinnamon, and nutmeg in a bowl. Cut the butter into small pieces, then add to the bowl and rub it in with your fingertips until the mixture resembles fine breadcrumbs.

For the batter, add the baking soda to the applesauce and stir until dissolved. Place the butter and raw brown sugar in a large bowl and beat together until light and fluffy. Gradually beat in the egg. Sift in the flour, cinnamon, and nutmeg and, using a metal spoon, fold into the batter, alternating with the applesauce.

Spoon the batter into the paper liners. Scatter the topping over the cupcakes and press down gently. Bake in the preheated oven for 20 minutes, or until risen, golden, and firm to the touch. Transfer to a wire rack and let cool.

Pistachio Cupcakes

MAKES 16

2/3 cup shelled, unsalted pistachio nuts

1/2 cup butter, softened, or soft margarine

3/4 cup superfine sugar

generous 1 cup self-rising flour

2 eggs, lightly beaten

1/4 cup Greek-style yogurt

1 tbsp chopped pistachio nuts, to decorate

BUTTERCREAM

1/2 cup unsalted butter, softened

2 tbsp lime juice syrup

green food coloring (optional)

1 2/3 cups confectioners' sugar

Preheat the oven to 350°/180°C. Put 16 paper liners into shallow muffin pans.

Put the pistachio nuts in a food processor or blender and process for a few seconds until finely ground. Add the butter, superfine sugar, flour, eggs, and yogurt and then process until evenly mixed.

Spoon the batter into the paper liners. Bake in the preheated oven for 20–25 minutes, or until risen, golden, and firm to the touch. Transfer to a wire rack and let cool.

To make the buttercream, put the butter, syrup, and a little green food coloring, if using, into a bowl and beat until fluffy. Sift in the confectioners' sugar and beat until smooth. Swirl the buttercream over the cupcakes and decorate with the chopped pistachio nuts.

Pure Indulgence Almond Cupcakes

MAKES 12

7 tbsp butter, softened, or soft margarine

½ cup superfine sugar

2 eggs, lightly beaten

¼ tsp almond extract

4 tbsp light cream

1⅓ cups all-purpose flour

1½ tsp baking powder

¾ cup ground almonds

toasted slivered almonds, to decorate

BUTTERCREAM

½ cup unsalted butter, softened

generous 1¾ cups confectioners' sugar

a few drops of almond extract

Preheat the oven to 350°/180°C. Put 12 paper liners into a muffin pan.

Place the butter and superfine sugar in a large bowl and beat together until light and fluffy. Gradually beat in the eggs, then add the almond extract and cream. Sift in the flour and baking powder and, using a metal spoon, fold into the batter with the ground almonds.

Spoon the batter into the paper liners. Bake in the preheated oven for 25 minutes, or until risen, golden, and firm to the touch. Transfer to a wire rack and let cool.

To make the buttercream, place the butter in a large bowl and beat until creamy. Sift in the confectioners' sugar, add the almond extract, and beat together until smooth. Spread the buttercream over the cupcakes and decorate with slivered almonds.

Tropical Pineapple Cupcakes

MAKES 12

2 canned pineapple rings

6 tbsp butter, softened,
or soft margarine

scant ½ cup superfine
sugar

1 extra large egg,
lightly beaten

⅔ cup self-rising flour

FROSTING

2 tbsp unsalted butter,
softened

scant ½ cup cream cheese

grated rind of 1 lemon
or lime

¾ cup confectioners' sugar

about 1 tsp lemon juice
or lime juice

Preheat the oven to 350°/180°C. Put 12 paper liners into a shallow muffin pan.

Drain the pineapple, reserving 1 tablespoon of the juice. Finely chop the pineapple. Place the butter and superfine sugar in a large bowl and beat together until light and fluffy. Gradually beat in the egg. Sift in the flour and, using a large metal spoon, fold into the batter. Fold in the chopped pineapple and the reserved pineapple juice.

Spoon the batter into the paper liners. Bake in the preheated oven for 20 minutes, or until risen, golden, and firm to the touch. Transfer to a wire rack and let cool.

To make the frosting, put the butter and cream cheese in a bowl and beat together until smooth. Add the lemon rind. Sift the confectioners' sugar into the mixture, then beat together until well mixed. Gradually beat in the lemon juice, adding enough to form a spreading consistency.

Spoon the frosting into a pastry bag fitted with a large star tip. Pipe a swirl of frosting on top of each cupcake.

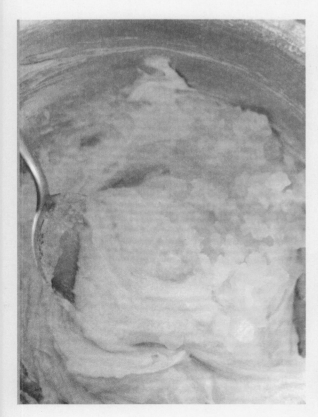

Maple Pecan Cupcakes

MAKES 30

1⅓ cups all-purpose flour

1 tbsp baking powder

¾ cup butter, softened, or soft margarine

generous ½ cup light brown sugar

4 tbsp maple syrup

3 eggs, lightly beaten

1 tsp vanilla extract

¼ cup finely chopped pecans

TOPPING

⅓ cup finely chopped pecans

2 tbsp all-purpose flour

2 tbsp light brown sugar

2 tbsp melted butter

Preheat the oven to 375°F/190°C. Put 30 paper liners into shallow muffin pans.

Sift the flour and baking powder into a large bowl. Add the butter, brown sugar, maple syrup, eggs, and vanilla extract and, using an electric mixer, beat together until smooth. Stir in the pecans.

Spoon the batter into the paper liners. To make the topping, mix together the pecans, flour, brown sugar, and melted butter to make a crumbly mixture and spoon a little on top of each cupcake.

Bake in the preheated oven for 15–20 minutes, or until risen, golden, and firm to the touch. Transfer to a wire rack and let cool.

Lemon Cornmeal Cupcakes

MAKES 14

½ cup butter, softened, or soft margarine

generous ½ cup superfine sugar

finely grated rind and juice of ½ lemon

2 eggs, lightly beaten

scant ½ cup all-purpose flour

1 tsp baking powder

¼ cup instant cornmeal

14 candied violets, to decorate

FROSTING

5½ oz/150 g mascarpone cheese

3 tbsp confectioners' sugar

2 tsp finely grated lemon rind

Preheat the oven to 350°/180°C. Put 14 paper liners into shallow muffin pans.

Place the butter and superfine sugar in a large bowl and beat together until light and fluffy. Beat in the lemon rind and juice. Gradually beat in the eggs. Sift in the flour and baking powder and, using a metal spoon, fold gently into the batter with the cornmeal.

Spoon the batter into the paper liners. Bake in the preheated oven for 20 minutes, or until risen, golden, and firm to the touch. Transfer to a wire rack and let cool.

To make the frosting, beat the mascarpone cheese until smooth. Sift in the confectioners' sugar, add the lemon rind, and beat together until well mixed. Spread the frosting over the cupcakes and decorate with candied violets.

Shredded Orange Cupcakes

MAKES 12

6 tbsp butter, softened, or soft margarine

scant ½ cup superfine sugar

1 extra large egg, lightly beaten

⅔ cup self-rising flour

¼ cup ground almonds

juice and grated rind of 1 small orange

2 tbsp toasted slivered almonds, to decorate

ORANGE SYRUP

juice and grated rind of 1 small orange

¼ cup superfine sugar

Preheat the oven to 350°/180°C. Put 12 paper liners into a shallow muffin pan.

Place the butter and superfine sugar in a bowl and beat together until light and fluffy. Gradually beat in the egg. Sift in the flour and, using a large metal spoon, fold into the batter with the ground almonds. Fold in the orange juice and rind.

Spoon the batter into the paper liners. Bake in the preheated oven for 20–25 minutes, or until risen, golden, and firm to the touch.

Meanwhile, make the orange syrup. Put the orange juice, orange rind, and superfine sugar into a saucepan and heat gently, stirring, until the sugar has dissolved, then simmer for 5 minutes.

Prick the tops of the warm cupcakes all over with a skewer and spoon over the orange syrup. Scatter the slivered almonds on top. Transfer to a wire rack and let cool.

I ♥ You Cupcakes

MAKES 10

½ cup butter, softened, or soft margarine

generous ½ cup superfine sugar

1 tsp almond extract

2 extra large eggs, lightly beaten

generous ½ cup self-rising flour

¼ cup ground almonds

2 tbsp milk

3 tbsp raspberry jelly

TO DECORATE

2¾ oz/75 g red ready-to-use fondant

5½ oz/150 g white ready-to-use fondant

1 tbsp egg white, lightly beaten

⅔ cup confectioners' sugar, sifted, plus extra for dusting

Preheat the oven to 350°F/180°C. Put 10 paper liners into a muffin pan.

Place the butter, superfine sugar, and almond extract in a large bowl and beat together until light and fluffy. Gradually beat in the eggs. Sift in the flour and, using a metal spoon, fold in gently with the ground almonds. Add the milk and fold gently into the batter.

Spoon the batter into the paper liners. Bake in the preheated oven for 20–25 minutes, until risen, golden, and firm to the touch. Transfer to a wire rack and let cool.

Using a small knife, scoop out a little of the cake from each cupcake. Place ½ teaspoon of the jelly into each hollow and replace the piece of cake on top.

Roll out a small piece of the red fondant and, using a small heart cutter, stamp out two hearts. Lightly knead the remaining red fondant into the white fondant to create a marbled effect. Roll out to a thickness of ¼ inch/5 mm on a surface lightly dusted with confectioners' sugar. Use a 2¾-inch/7-cm cutter to stamp out 10 rounds. Brush the top of the cupcakes with the remaining jelly and place the fondant rounds on top.

Place the egg white in a bowl and gradually beat in the confectioners' sugar to make a smooth icing. Spoon the icing into a small pastry bag fitted with a fine writing tip. Pipe each of the letters I, Y, O, and U on two cupcakes and attach the fondant hearts with a dab of water to the two remaining cupcakes.

Valentine Heart Cupcakes

MAKES 6

6 tbsp butter, softened, or soft margarine

scant ½ cup superfine sugar

½ tsp vanilla extract

2 eggs, lightly beaten

generous ½ cup all-purpose flour

1 tbsp unsweetened cocoa

1 tsp baking powder

6 sugar flowers, to decorate

MARZIPAN HEARTS

1¼ oz/35 g marzipan

red food coloring

confectioners' sugar, for dusting

FROSTING

4 tbsp unsalted butter, softened

scant 1 cup confectioners' sugar

1 oz/25 g semisweet chocolate, melted

To make the marzipan hearts, knead the marzipan until pliable, then add a little food coloring and knead until evenly colored. Roll out the marzipan to a thickness of ¼ inch/5 mm on a surface lightly dusted with confectioners' sugar. Using a small heart cutter, cut out six hearts. Place on a sheet of wax paper dusted with confectioners' sugar and let dry for 3–4 hours.

Preheat the oven to 350°F/180°C. Put 6 paper liners into a muffin pan.

Place the butter, superfine sugar, and vanilla extract in a large bowl and beat together until light and fluffy. Gradually beat in the eggs. Sift in the flour, cocoa, and baking powder and, using a metal spoon, fold into the batter.

Spoon the batter into the paper liners. Bake in the preheated oven for 20–25 minutes, or until risen and firm to the touch. Transfer to a wire rack and let cool.

To make the frosting, put the butter in a large bowl and beat until fluffy. Sift in the confectioners' sugar and beat together until smooth. Add the melted chocolate and beat together until well mixed. Spread some of the frosting on top of each cupcake and decorate with a marzipan heart and sugar flower.

Rose Petal Cupcakes

MAKES 12

½ cup butter, softened, or soft margarine

generous ½ cup superfine sugar

2 eggs, lightly beaten

1⅓ cups self-rising flour

1 tbsp milk

a few drops of rose oil essence

¼ tsp vanilla extract

sugar-frosted rose petals, to decorate (see page 42)

BUTTERCREAM

6 tbsp unsalted butter, softened

1⅓ cups confectioners' sugar

pink food coloring (optional)

Preheat the oven to 400°F/200°C. Put 12 paper liners into a shallow muffin pan.

Place the butter and superfine sugar in a large bowl and beat together until light and fluffy. Gradually beat in the eggs. Sift in the flour and, using a metal spoon, fold in gently. Stir in the milk, rose oil essence, and vanilla extract.

Spoon the batter into the paper liners. Bake in the preheated oven for 12–15 minutes, until risen, golden, and firm to the touch. Transfer to a wire rack and let cool.

To make the buttercream, put the butter in a large bowl and beat until fluffy. Sift in the confectioners' sugar and mix well together. Add a little pink food coloring, if using, to give a pale pink color.

Spoon the buttercream into a pastry bag fitted with a large plain tip. Pipe a dollop of buttercream on top of each cupcake and decorate with sugar-frosted rose petals.

Wedding Cupcakes

MAKES 30

2¾ cups self-rising flour

1 tsp baking powder

1 cup butter, softened, or soft margarine

heaping 1 cup superfine sugar

finely grated rind of 1 large lemon

4 extra large eggs, lightly beaten

2 tbsp milk

TO DECORATE

1 lb 7 oz/650 g white ready-to-use fondant

3 tbsp apricot jelly, warmed, or apricot preserve, warmed and strained

15 white fondant roses, dipped in edible silver glitter (see page 40)

2 tbsp egg white, lightly beaten

1¼ cups confectioners' sugar, sifted, plus extra for dusting

Preheat the oven to 325°F/160°C. Put 30 paper liners into shallow muffin pans.

Sift the flour and baking powder into a large bowl. Add the butter, superfine sugar, lemon rind, eggs, and milk and, using an electric mixer, beat together until smooth.

Spoon the batter into the paper liners. Bake in the preheated oven for 20–25 minutes, until risen, golden, and firm to the touch. Transfer to a wire rack and let cool.

Roll out the white fondant to a thickness of ¼ inch/ 5 mm on a surface lightly dusted with confectioners' sugar. Using a 2½-inch/6-cm cutter, stamp out 30 rounds, rerolling the fondant as necessary. Brush each cupcake lightly with a little of the jelly and gently press a fondant round on top. Gently press a fondant rose into the center of half of the fondant-topped cupcakes.

Place the egg white in a bowl and gradually beat in the confectioners' sugar to make a smooth icing. Spoon the icing into a small pastry bag fitted with a fine writing tip. Starting at an edge, pipe a random meandering line of icing all over the surface of each plain cupcake. Try not to let the lines touch or cross and keep an even pressure on the pastry bag so that the lines are of the same thickness. Let set.

Silver or Golden Anniversary Cupcakes

MAKES 24

1 cup butter, softened, or soft margarine

generous 1 cup superfine sugar

4 extra large eggs, lightly beaten

1 tsp vanilla extract

1¾ cups self-rising flour

5 tbsp milk

silver or gold dragées, to decorate

BUTTERCREAM

¾ cup unsalted butter, softened

2¾ cups confectioners' sugar

Preheat the oven to 350°F/180°C. Put 24 silver or gold foil liners into shallow muffin pans.

Place the butter and superfine sugar in a large bowl and beat together until light and fluffy. Gradually beat in the eggs and vanilla extract. Sift in the flour and, using a large metal spoon, fold into the batter with the milk.

Spoon the batter into the foil liners. Bake in the preheated oven for 15–20 minutes, or until risen, golden, and firm to the touch. Transfer to a wire rack and let cool.

To make the buttercream, put the butter in a bowl and beat until fluffy. Sift in the confectioners' sugar and beat together until smooth.

Spoon the buttercream into a pastry bag fitted with a star tip. Pipe swirls of buttercream on top of each cupcake and decorate with dragées.

Birthday Party Cupcakes

MAKES 24

1¾ cups self-rising flour

1 cup butter, softened,
or soft margarine

generous 1 cup superfine
sugar

4 eggs, lightly beaten

BUTTERCREAM

¾ cup unsalted butter,
softened

2¾ cups confectioners'
sugar

TO DECORATE

sugar sprinkles and sugar
flowers

candles and candle holders
(optional)

Preheat the oven to 350°F/180°C. Put 24 paper liners into shallow muffin pans.

Sift the flour into a large bowl. Add the butter, superfine sugar, and eggs and, using an electric mixer, beat together until smooth.

Spoon the batter into the paper liners. Bake in the preheated oven for 15–20 minutes, or until risen, golden, and firm to the touch. Transfer to a wire rack and let cool.

To make the buttercream, put the butter in a bowl and beat until fluffy. Sift in the confectioners' sugar and beat together until smooth and creamy.

Spoon the buttercream into a pastry bag fitted with a large star tip. Pipe swirls of buttercream on top of each cupcake and decorate with sugar sprinkles and sugar flowers. If using, place a candle in a candle holder on the top of each.

New Baby Cupcakes

MAKES 12

scant 1 cup self-rising flour

¼ tsp baking powder

½ cup butter, softened, or soft margarine

generous ½ cup superfine sugar

2 eggs, lightly beaten

1 tbsp milk

1 tsp vanilla extract

TO DECORATE

5½ oz/150 g white ready-to-use fondant

confectioners' sugar, for dusting

5½ oz/150 g pale blue or pink ready-to-use fondant

1 tbsp apricot jelly, warmed, or apricot preserve, warmed and strained

tube of white writing icing

Preheat the oven to 350°F/180°C. Put 12 paper liners into a shallow muffin pan.

Sift the flour and baking powder into a large bowl. Add the butter, superfine sugar, eggs, milk, and vanilla extract and, using an electric mixer, beat together until smooth.

Spoon the batter into the paper liners. Bake in the preheated oven for 15–20 minutes, until risen, golden, and firm to the touch. Transfer to a wire rack and let cool.

Roll out the white fondant to a thickness of ¼ inch/ 5 mm on a surface lightly dusted with confectioners' sugar. Using a 2½-inch/6-cm cutter, stamp out 6 rounds. Repeat with the blue or pink fondant. Brush each cupcake lightly with a little of the jelly and gently press a fondant round on top.

Reroll the blue or pink fondant trimmings. Use a small teddy bear cutter to stamp out 2 teddy bears. Use a tiny flower cutter to stamp out 4 flowers. Reroll the white fondant trimmings. Use a small flower cutter to stamp out 2 small flowers. Use a 1½-inch/4-cm fluted cutter to stamp out 2 rounds, then cut away a small oval from each round to resemble a baby's bib. Use a 1-inch/2.5-cm cutter to stamp out 2 rounds and mark with the end of a paintbrush to resemble buttons. Shape 4 booties and 2 ducks from the remaining fondant trimmings.

Attach all the decorations to the top of the cupcakes with a little water. Use the writing icing to add the finishing touches, such as bows on the booties.

Easter Cupcakes

MAKES 12

1/2 cup butter, softened, or soft margarine

generous 1/2 cup superfine sugar

2 eggs, lightly beaten

2/3 cup self-rising flour

1/4 cup unsweetened cocoa

36 miniature candy-covered chocolate eggs, to decorate

BUTTERCREAM

6 tbsp unsalted butter, softened

1 1/3 cups confectioners' sugar

1 tbsp milk

a few drops of vanilla extract

Preheat the oven to 350°F/180°C. Put 12 paper liners into a shallow muffin pan.

Place the butter and superfine sugar in a large bowl and beat together until light and fluffy. Gradually beat in the eggs. Sift in the flour and cocoa and, using a metal spoon, fold into the batter.

Spoon the batter into the paper liners. Bake in the preheated oven for 15–20 minutes, or until risen and firm to the touch. Transfer to a wire rack and let cool.

To make the buttercream, put the unsalted butter into a bowl and beat until fluffy. Sift in the confectioners' sugar and beat together until well mixed, adding the milk and vanilla extract.

Spoon the buttercream into a pastry bag fitted with a large star tip. Pipe a circle of buttercream on top of each cupcake to form a nest. Place 3 candy-covered chocolate eggs in the center of each nest to decorate.

Marzipan Flower Cupcakes

MAKES 12

scant 1 cup self-rising flour

½ tsp baking powder

½ cup butter, softened, or soft margarine

generous ½ cup superfine sugar

2 eggs, lightly beaten

a few drops of almond extract

TO DECORATE

7 oz/200 g marzipan

confectioners' sugar, for dusting

2 tbsp apricot jelly, warmed, or apricot preserve, warmed and strained

Preheat the oven to 350°F/180°C. Put 12 paper liners into a shallow muffin pan.

Sift the flour and baking powder into a large bowl. Add the butter, superfine sugar, eggs, and almond extract and, using an electric mixer, beat together until smooth.

Spoon the batter into the paper liners. Bake in the preheated oven for 20 minutes, or until risen, golden, and firm to the touch. Transfer to a wire rack and let cool.

Roll out the marzipan on a surface lightly dusted with confectioners' sugar. Using a 1¼-inch/3-cm cutter, stamp out 60 rounds, rerolling the marzipan as necessary. Spread a little jelly over the top of each cupcake. Pinch the marzipan circles at one side to create petal shapes and arrange 5 petals on top of each cupcake. Roll the remaining marzipan into 12 small balls for the flower centers and place in the middle of the cupcakes.

Candy Store Cupcakes

MAKES 12

scant ¾ cup butter, softened, or soft margarine

¾ cup superfine sugar

3 eggs, lightly beaten

1¼ cups self-rising flour

4 tsp strawberry-flavored popping candy

candies of your choice, to decorate

BUTTERCREAM

¾ cup unsalted butter, softened

2 tbsp milk

2¾ cups confectioners' sugar

pink and yellow food coloring

Preheat the oven to 350°F/180°C. Put 12 paper liners into a shallow muffin pan.

Place the butter and superfine sugar in a large bowl and beat together until light and fluffy. Gradually beat in the eggs. Sift in the flour and, using a metal spoon, fold in gently. Fold in half of the popping candy.

Spoon the batter into the paper liners. Bake in the preheated oven for 18–22 minutes, until risen, golden, and firm to the touch. Transfer to a wire rack and let cool.

To make the buttercream, place the butter in a bowl and beat with an electric mixer for 2–3 minutes, until pale and creamy. Beat in the milk, then gradually sift in the confectioners' sugar and continue beating for 2–3 minutes, until the buttercream is light and fluffy. Divide the buttercream between two bowls and beat a little pink or yellow food coloring into each bowl.

Pipe or swirl the buttercream on top of the cupcakes and decorate with candies. Sprinkle over the remaining popping candy just before serving.

Caramel Apple Cupcakes

MAKES 16

2 apples

1 tbsp lemon juice

2 cups all-purpose flour

2 tsp baking powder

1½ tsp ground cinnamon

⅓ cup light brown sugar

4 tbsp butter, melted, plus extra for greasing

scant ½ cup milk

scant ½ cup apple juice

1 egg, lightly beaten

CARAMEL SAUCE

2 tbsp heavy cream

scant ¼ cup light brown sugar

1 tbsp butter

Preheat the oven to 400°F/200°C. Grease 16 cups in two shallow muffin pans.

Roughly grate 1 apple. Cut the remaining apple into ¼-inch/5-mm-thick slices and toss in the lemon juice. Sift the flour, baking powder, and cinnamon into a large bowl, then stir in the brown sugar and grated apple.

Combine the melted butter with the milk, apple juice, and egg. Stir the liquid ingredients into the dry ingredients, mixing lightly until just combined.

Spoon the batter into the prepared pans and arrange 2 of the apple slices on top of each cupcake. Bake in the preheated oven for 15–20 minutes, or until risen, golden, and firm to the touch. Transfer to a wire rack and let cool.

For the caramel sauce, place all the ingredients in a small saucepan and heat, stirring, until the sugar is dissolved. Increase the heat and boil rapidly for 2 minutes, or until slightly thickened and syrupy. Cool slightly, then drizzle over the cupcakes and let set.

Halloween Spider Cupcakes

MAKES 12

scant 1 cup self-rising flour

½ cup butter, softened, or soft margarine

generous ½ cup superfine sugar

2 eggs, lightly beaten

TO DECORATE

7 oz/200 g orange ready-to-use fondant

confectioners' sugar, for dusting

2 oz/55 g black ready-to-use fondant

tubes of black and yellow writing icing

Preheat the oven to 350°F/180°C. Put 12 paper liners into a shallow muffin pan.

Sift the flour into a large bowl. Add the butter, superfine sugar, and eggs and, using an electric mixer, beat together until smooth.

Spoon the batter into the paper liners. Bake in the preheated oven for 15–20 minutes, or until risen, golden, and firm to the touch. Transfer to a wire rack and let cool.

Roll out the orange fondant to a thickness of ¼ inch/5 mm on a surface lightly dusted with confectioners' sugar. Using a 2¼-inch/5.5-cm plain cutter, stamp out 12 rounds, rerolling the fondant as necessary. Place a fondant round on top of each cupcake.

Roll out the black fondant to the same thickness. Using a 1¼-inch/3-cm plain cutter, cut out 12 rounds and place 1 round on the center of each cupcake. Using black writing icing, pipe 8 legs onto each spider and, using yellow writing icing, pipe 2 eyes and a mouth.

Ghostly Ghoul Cupcakes

MAKES 6

6 tbsp butter, softened, or soft margarine

scant ½ cup dark brown sugar

1 tbsp molasses

2 extra large eggs, lightly beaten

generous 1 cup all-purpose flour

2 tsp ground allspice

¾ tsp baking soda

BUTTERCREAM

6 tbsp unsalted butter, softened

1 tbsp dulce de leche or caramel sauce

1⅓ cups confectioners' sugar

TO DECORATE

12 oz/350 g white ready-to-use fondant

confectioners' sugar, for dusting

tube of black writing icing

Preheat the oven to 350°F/180°C. Put 12 paper liners into a shallow muffin pan and 6 paper liners into a miniature muffin pan.

Place the butter, brown sugar, and molasses in a bowl and beat together until light and fluffy. Gradually beat in the eggs. Sift in the flour, allspice, and baking soda and, using a metal spoon, fold in gently.

Spoon the batter into the paper liners. Bake the mini muffins in the preheated oven for 10–12 minutes and the cupcakes for 15–20 minutes, until risen and firm to the touch. Transfer to a wire rack and let cool.

To make the buttercream, place the butter and dulce de leche in a bowl and beat with an electric mixer for 2–3 minutes, until pale and creamy. Gradually sift in the confectioners' sugar and beat until smooth.

To assemble, remove the paper liners from half of the cupcakes and all the mini muffins. Level the tops of all the cakes, if necessary. Spread a layer of buttercream over the top of the remaining cupcakes. Top each with an upturned cupcake and an upturned mini muffin. Spread the buttercream all over the stacked cakes. Chill in the refrigerator for 30 minutes.

Take 1¾ oz/50 g of the white fondant and roll into 6 small balls. Place a ball on top of each of the stacked cakes. Divide the remaining fondant into 6 pieces and roll out each piece on a surface lightly dusted with confectioners' sugar to a 5½-inch/14-cm round with a thickness of about ⅛ inch/3 mm. Drape over the cupcakes. Use the black writing icing to pipe ghost faces on each cupcake.

Festive Holly Cupcakes

MAKES 16

generous ½ cup butter, softened, or soft margarine

1 cup superfine sugar

4 eggs, lightly beaten

a few drops of almond extract

1¼ cups self-rising flour

1¾ cups ground almonds

TO DECORATE

1 lb/450 g white ready-to-use fondant

confectioners' sugar, for dusting

2 oz/55 g green ready-to-use fondant

1 oz/25 g red ready-to-use fondant

Preheat the oven to 350°F/180°C. Put 16 paper liners into a muffin pan.

Place the butter and superfine sugar in a large bowl and beat together until light and fluffy. Gradually beat in the eggs and almond extract. Sift in the flour and, using a metal spoon, fold into the batter with the ground almonds.

Spoon the batter into the paper liners. Bake in the preheated oven for 20 minutes, or until risen, golden, and firm to the touch. Transfer to a wire rack and let cool.

Roll out the white fondant to a thickness of ¼ inch/ 5 mm on a surface lightly dusted with confectioners' sugar. Using a 2¾-inch/7-cm plain cutter, stamp out 16 rounds, rerolling the icing as necessary. Place a fondant round on top of each cupcake.

Roll out the green fondant to the same thickness. Using a holly cutter, cut out 32 leaves, rerolling the fondant as necessary. Brush each leaf with a little water and place 2 leaves on top of each cupcake. Roll the red fondant to form 48 small berries and place on the leaves.

Christmas Star Cupcakes

MAKES 12

6 tbsp butter, softened, or soft margarine

scant ½ cup light brown sugar

1 extra large egg, lightly beaten

⅔ cup self-rising flour

½ tsp ground cinnamon

1 tbsp milk

GOLD STARS

3 oz/85 g yellow ready-to-use fondant

confectioners' sugar, for dusting

edible gold glitter (optional)

ICING

⅔ cup confectioners' sugar

2–3 tsp lemon juice

Preheat the oven to 350°F/180°C. Put 12 paper liners into a shallow muffin pan.

Place the butter and brown sugar in a large bowl and beat together until light and fluffy. Gradually beat in the egg. Sift in the flour and cinnamon and, using a metal spoon, fold into the batter with the milk.

Spoon the batter into the paper liners. Bake in the preheated oven for 20 minutes, or until risen, golden, and firm to the touch. Transfer to a wire rack and let cool.

To make the gold stars, roll out the yellow fondant to a thickness of ¼ inch/5 mm on a surface lightly dusted with confectioners' sugar. Using a small star cutter, stamp out 12 stars. Brush each star with a little gold glitter, if using. Set aside on a sheet of parchment paper.

To make the icing, sift the confectioners' sugar into a bowl and stir in enough of the lemon juice to make a smooth, thick icing.

Spoon the icing over the cupcakes and top each with a gold star. Let set.

Snowman Cupcakes

MAKES 10

½ cup butter, softened, or soft margarine

generous ½ cup superfine sugar

2 extra large eggs, lightly beaten

scant 1 cup self-rising flour

scant 1 cup unsweetened dried shredded coconut

2 tbsp milk

BUTTERCREAM

4 tbsp unsalted butter, softened

2 tbsp heavy cream

scant 1 cup confectioners' sugar

TO DECORATE

2 oz/55 g black ready-to-roll fondant

confectioners' sugar, for dusting

candied cherries, angelica, chocolate chips, and orange jelly diamonds

Preheat the oven to 350°F/180°C. Put 10 paper liners into a shallow muffin pan.

Place the butter and superfine sugar in a large bowl and beat together until light and fluffy. Gradually beat in the eggs. Sift in the flour and, using a metal spoon, fold in gently. Fold in a generous ½ cup of the coconut and the milk.

Spoon the batter into the paper liners. Bake in the preheated oven for 15–20 minutes, until risen, golden, and firm to the touch. Transfer to a wire rack and let cool.

To make the buttercream, place the butter in a bowl and beat with an electric mixer for 2–3 minutes, until pale and creamy. Beat in the cream, then gradually sift in the confectioners' sugar and continue beating for 2–3 minutes, until the buttercream is light and fluffy.

Spread the buttercream over the cupcakes, using a palette knife to smooth and shape it into a slight mound. Sprinkle over the remaining coconut.

Roll out the black fondant on a surface lightly dusted with confectioners' sugar and cut out 10 hat shapes. Decorate each hat with small pieces of candied cherry and angelica to resemble holly leaves and berries. Place on the cupcakes. Gently press 2 chocolate chips, a piece of jelly diamond, and a rolled strip of black fondant on top of each cupcake for the snowman's eyes, nose, and mouth.

Index

Happy baking!